It All Starts with a Smile

the LAUGH DOCTOR™

It All Starts with a Smile

7 Steps To Being Happier Right Now

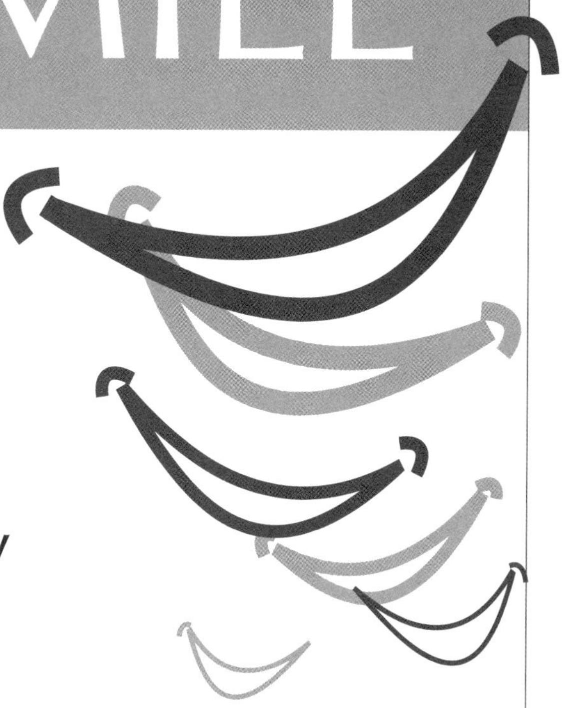

the LAUGH DOCTOR™

Clifford Kuhn, M.D.

This book has not been a solitary enterprise. Every page reflects the input and guidance of friends and patients too numerous to mention individually. Nonetheless, I am grateful to each of you.

Special thanks go to my business and marketing guru, Deborah Lanore, without whose energy, vision and perseverance there would be no book.

I am also grateful to Linda Cashden, our editor, whose expertise and commitment were above and beyond all reasonable expectations.

My son, Greg, deserves recognition for his contributions. Not only did he submit many of the ideas contained on these pages, but he tirelessly poured over the manuscript, adding his own re-writes, some of which he allowed me to include verbatim. I could not ask for a more creative and inspirational collaborator.

My deepest gratitude is reserved for Constance, my wife, best friend and heart mate. Her loving spirit is a sustained and unerring beacon of joy that lights my path.

BUTLER BOOKS LOUISVILLE, KY

ISBN 1-884532-90-X
Printed in Canada
Book design by Eric Butler

For information, contact the publisher:
Butler Books
P.O. Box 7311
Louisville, KY 40207
502-897-9393/Fax 502-897-9797
www.butlerbooks.com

CONTENTS

Introduction 3

• SECTION 1 •
HA: *Adjusting Your Humor Attitude*

Step One:
DIAGNOSE THE PROBLEM 7

Step Two:
PLAY TO WIN, REJECT VICTIMHOOD 33

Step Three:
CHOOSE FUN OVER FUNNY 59

• SECTION 2 •
HA HA: *Rediscovering Your Humor Aptitude*

Step Four:
UNLEASH YOUR HUMOR NATURE 79

Step Five:
PRACTICE THE SMILE STRATEGIES 101

CONTENTS

• SECTION 3 •

HA HA HA: *Practicing Your Humor Action*

Step Six:
DO SOMETHING...NOW! 151

Step Seven:
IMPROVE WITH IMPROV 175

Post Script:
KEEPING IT FRESH 196

Introduction

The middle-aged CEO sat dejectedly in my consulting room. It was mid-morning, but he had the look of a weary man who had already put in a full day's work. His attire reflected expensive tastes and the wealth to indulge them.

"I thought when I got to this point in life I'd be happy," he said hoarsely. "I'm making more money than I ever imagined. I've got three homes, a beautiful wife, great kids and expensive toys I can't even find the time to play with.

"I'm a successful man," he insisted. "I should be free to do whatever I want. But I can't get free. I have no time to enjoy any of it. It feels like I'm on a treadmill and I can't get off. I'm trapped by my success and I'm not happy."

Tears welled up in his eyes. Embarrassed, he looked furtively around my office. "Where the hell are your tissues?" he grumbled. "You're a shrink, for God's sake. Surely you have a tissue."

"Do you want a new one or a used one?" I asked.

He looked at me sharply.

"The new ones cost extra," I said, keeping a straight face.

He looked confused. Then I saw a light of recognition in his eyes, and he burst into a laugh that lasted longer than my silly joke warranted. When he caught his breath, he had a very different kind of tears in his eyes.

"That's the first good laugh I've had this week," he said. "I used to laugh all the time. That's what's missing!"

"Sounds like you're not having any fun," I ventured.

"Damn right! That's why I'm here. You're the Laugh Doctor, after all. I want you to fix me."

I am the laugh doctor, a psychiatrist who for decades now has researched humor's physiological and psychological powers. A professor and former Associate Chairman of the University of Louisville Medical School's Department of Psychiatry, I have studied the healing effects of laughter from an academic perspective, from my own medical case studies, and from working (and playing) with such world famous humor practitioners as comedian Jerry Lewis, Dr. Patch Adams, about whose life a successful movie has been made, Allen Klein, best-selling author and past president of the Association for Applied and Therapeutic humor, Dr. Steve Wilson, the founder and guiding spirit of The World Laughter Tour, and "Doc Hollywood" himself, Dr. Neil Shulman.

This research has enabled me to develop my own highly successful HA HA HA Prescription, which is designed to capitalize on laughter's ability to heal, and to witness the beneficial effects of the HA HA HA Prescription in my medical practice. I have had the pleasure, for example, of accompanying one patient, "Judy," on a triumphant fun-filled trip months after her predicted death from a recurrent untreatable cancer. I have rejoiced with another patient, "Robert"—a previously serious person—who, given only a 50 percent chance of surviving five years with his tumor, dedicated himself to daily laughter and recently celebrated his twelfth cancer-free year.

We know that humor's natural healing power lies in its ability to quickly and effectively dissipate stress, the number one destroyer of human health. Medical studies have demonstrated that stress causes high blood pressure, muscle tension, and even suppresses the body's immune system.

Laughter and the positive emotions laughter generates, on the other hand, have been found to boost the immune system, stabilize blood pressure, massage inner organs, stimulate circulation, and increase the flow of oxygen to the muscles, thereby decreasing tension.

How, then, do we go about generating more laughter in our lives? How can people maintain a sense of humor when they are fearful or depressed, anxious, physically uncomfortable, over worked, in pain, or uncertain about the future?

I have an answer—my HA HA HA Prescription, a three-phase formula for unleashing the marvelous healing power of your humor nature in every situation. The three HA'S stand for Humor Attitude, Humor Aptitude, and Humor Action. Followed in proper order, they are the keys to restoring the full measure of this natural medicine. The book will guide you through this sequence.

Section I will focus on adjusting your humor attitude, which creates the foundation for lifelong benefits. You will see how you have come to disparage and even trivialize humor, and then find ample support and lots of encouragement for adopting a more respectful disposition toward your most magnificent gift.

Section II deals with the rediscovery of your natural ability to have fun. You will be happy to find that you have not lost your inborn talent for humor, despite, in some cases, years of neglect and misuse. Nothing new will be required, but you may have to brush a few cobwebs off some things you once knew and have since forgotten. Like riding a bicycle, your ability to have fun will return once you work to bring it back, and you will forget you ever lost it.

Finally, Section III will teach you specific activities that are designed to enhance the presence of fun and laughter in your life, so that you can enjoy the benefits any time and anywhere. You will be introduced to the tactics used by successful comedy professionals to release humor's energy, and keep it fresh and strong day after day. You will see that you don't have to be a "comedian" yourself to put these tactics into practice. They are guaranteed to work for you because they will be rooted in the strong foundation of your newly revitalized humor attitude and aptitude.

Do you know what it would it take to make you happy? Do you think you could achieve the success you yearn for in your personal relations and in your work? Are you still searching for the joy and satisfaction you once envisioned for yourself, or have you given up hope of ever finding it?

People tell me that answering such questions honestly makes them uncomfortable. Many say they have tried so many elusive remedies they wonder whether anything could truly make them happy. Some have become disillusioned and frustrated by their inability to achieve personal or professional success. Others feel stymied by bad health. The fact is, increasing numbers of Americans today report dissatisfaction and lack of fulfillment in their work and a lack of joy in their lives.

We seem to have become a distressed and desperate people. The harder we strive to feel better about ourselves, the more discouraged we become when we can't capture that elusive state of mind.

This book is written to resolve that dilemma and to help us claim the health and vitality of a joy-filled existence. I guarantee its success. Read it and practice the seven steps it teaches and you will encounter a life of increased optimism, energy, and resilience. I am proud to share this life changing information with people all over the world. Its rapid success formula is just what the doctor ordered.

So, let's get started!

Step One: Diagnose the Problem

On his seventieth birthday, a man decided he wanted to live for a long time. He started to diet and exercise, and gave up smoking. He lost his gut, his body firmed up, and, to make the picture complete, he bought a toupee to cover his bald scalp.

Then he walked out in the street and was hit by the first car that came along.

As he lay dying, he called up, "God, how could you do this to me?"

God answered, "To tell you the truth, I didn't recognize you!"

Did you think that was funny? Did you laugh a little? Did you smile? Did you at least get a gleam in your eye or exhale an appreciative grunt? If so, you have just inoculated yourself against America's #1 threat to health: Stress.

Last year alone stress cost America more than 300 billion dollars in lost human productivity. At least 80 percent of the complaints you are bringing to your physician's office are stress induced or stress related. Every disease that is considered life threatening—cancer, heart disease, depression, etc.—has stress at its core. We are in a full-fledged epidemic of stress!

As you will learn later in this chapter, that smile, laugh, giggle, gleam or even appreciative grunt you just issued is the most powerful antidote to stress. But before we can discuss the cure, we need to understand the scope of the problem.

Stress is so rampant and ubiquitous that I have dubbed it the modern "black plague." Because it is so widespread, there is the very real danger that you will accept stress as a "normal" component of your modern lifestyle. We see evidence of this as we banter about such terms as "workplace stress," "eustress" (meaning stress that promotes constructive action), and "normal everyday stress."

I want to take an unequivocal and unflinching stand right now: ***There is no such thing as normal or acceptable stress!*** All stress is pathological and destructive, and thus the only constructive goal is its complete and total elimination. If you accept the notion that some stress is necessary and inevitable in your life, you have already succumbed to the epidemic and are probably suffering some of its consequences.

The cornerstone of all effective treatment plans—the basic tenet of all medicine, wherever it is practiced around the world—is an accurate diagnosis. Therefore, it is not enough to simply say that stress is the biggest enemy of your health and success. We must be more precise in illuminating the cause of the problem.

• FIND THE CAUSE •

As devastating as it is to your personal and corporate "health," stress, after all, is just a symptom—a signal or an alarm that exists to call attention to a potentially *more serious underlying problem.* We doctors consider it a mistake to treat a symptom, no matter how discomforting it may be, until it's true cause is identified and understood. Symptomatic treatment, without a "deeper" diagnosis, usually proves to be inadequate and in many cases dangerous, in that it may permit a continuing undetected proliferation of the underlying problem, to the further detriment of the patient.

Think of it this way: If the smoke alarm in your home goes off, would you:

Look around and "diagnose" what set it off *(IS THERE A FIRE?)*, making certain no danger could come to you or your family,

OR

Would you check the mechanism of the alarm to see whether it is suffering from a weak battery or poor connection?

I think we're all on the same page here. It would be just plain stupid to try to fix the alarm itself rather than taking steps to diagnose what it was that turned it on—and, if necessary, put out the fire.

That, however, is what you and I do about our stress. Instead of searching for the cause, we treat the symptom. When it is impossible to ignore your stress, you spend a great deal of time and money trying to tone it down or turn it off. Physical exercise becomes something you do, not for enjoyment, but as a means to "work off" tension. And then what do you do after exercising? You go right back to the very activities that produced your stress and begin re-accumulating dangerous levels of this killer!

It can be even worse when you choose to "medicate" your stress away. The pharmaceutical industry makes a fortune on stress reducing pills that some people end up gulping like daily vitamins. If you become dependent on the pills, you have added a second problem without solving the first.

The point is, "stress management" doesn't work because it deals with the symptoms of stress, not the cause—the problem at the root of your behavior.

You will notice something else as you look more carefully at stress. Above and beyond its being only a symptom and not a disease, it turns out it's not even real. That's right. Stress is a perception, the most subjective of all things. **Stress is your perception that you have no effective response to forces or events that are beyond your control.** Stress is truly in the "eye" of the beholder.

You are driving along on a beautiful morning, feeling on top of the world. The sun is shining, the birds are singing and you are singing right along with them. Suddenly you begin wondering whether you can get done all the errands you have planned and still pick up the kids on time from school. What if you can't? You envision them standing there, waiting alone after all the other children have left. Then, you picture a stranger driving up and offering them a ride. Your mouth goes dry. Your heart pumps faster. You get goose bumps. You can't hear the birds anymore and it feels like the sun has disappeared.

What you don't recognize is that all the reasons for the happiness you were enjoying a few seconds ago are still present and valid. And, further, the dreaded possibilities currently on your mind had already been possible during those previous moments of happiness. In other words, it was your focus upon one aspect of reality over another that determined your sudden shift of demeanor.

That's how stress works. It is the result of your mind telling your body that something is wrong and you are in danger and distress... and your body *believing it* enough to create a physical response to the message. Over time, your combined physical responses to such messages of doom can cause obesity, insomnia, high blood pressure, heart disease, a stroke, cancer, chronic pain, alcoholism and a plethora of other maladies.

Your mind is not intentionally stressing out your body. It is behaving exactly as it was taught. It actually believes the distressful message it is sending because, like all of us, you were trained and indoctrinated to take your thoughts very seriously. You were taught seriousness as you grew up. Those lessons were reinforced throughout your schooling, and your seriousness has been cemented as an adult.

So you see, there is, in fact, no such thing as objective, stand-alone stress. Stress is not a property of the environment. It just does not exist outside of you and me. That is why one person's stress may be another person's delight and a third person's tedium. You, and you alone, decide what's stressful for you, just as I choose my own stress.

Are you beginning to see yet another reason you are missing the boat on healing your stress?

How many times have you heard or read about "workplace stress" or "stressful life events," terms that imply stress is something occurring outside of you? The workplace has no stress. It has fears, uncertainties, and email. The stress is what you and I make of those things.

Can you see how the term "stress management," defining a huge industry dedicated to your welfare, can subtly misguide your focus?

When you are misled by such words to focus on what's outside of you, the best you can hope for is temporary, symptomatic relief of your stress.

Now we're getting somewhere, because we have uncovered a big clue as to the deeper cause of your killer stress. Since **stress is the result of your perception,** its cause can't be the economy, or worldwide terrorism, or even the Jerry Springer Show—as distressing as those things can be.

The cause of your stress is none other than you...and you alone. Don't ever underestimate the power of perception. It can isolate us from each other, or it can draw us closer together. It all depends on how we perceive ourselves in relation to the world around us. Is the glass half full or half empty?

Imagine us all standing on a beautiful beach, side-by-side with all of humanity. People are lined up as far as you can see in both directions. We're all holding hands while looking out over the lovely surf to witness the most gorgeous sunset ever. We're rendered breathless by its beauty. Picture the crimsons and golds and purples and pinks.

Just as the brilliant sun touches the horizon, you notice that a shimmering reflection of orange light is coming across the surface of the water and pointing directly at you.

You think to yourself, "How lucky I am, to be the one person in this entire group perfectly aligned with this beautiful shaft of light." You're feeling pretty special!

Your next thought is, "I wonder if any of the others are noticing whom the light is pointing to. I wonder if they are jealous."

Finally, you decide, "I better not say anything about it. It might make everyone else feel worse."

And, while you are entertaining that isolating thought, so is every other person on the beach.

Stress is the by-product of how we perceive ourselves in relation to everything else. To change your stress, you don't have to change your surroundings. All you have to do is change your perceptions.

That's why humor is so effective in eliminating stress. If you unleash it, it changes your perceptions. When your perceptions change, your stress changes immediately.

Perceptions are related to attitude. It is your attitude that determines whether you see a glass half full or half empty, or, for that matter, whether you look at the glass at all. So if your stress is your perception and your perception comes from your attitude, what attitude are you carrying around that produces such an uncomfortable and unhealthy effect?

That's the critical question and the answer comes from many years of study and research. I have learned that the perception that spawns your stress is actually a misperception (a mistake, if you will) that has been passed down to you from your earliest ancestors. *You and I have learned to take ourselves too seriously* and that is the root of all our stress.

I believe this mistake goes all the way back to the beginning of our species. Consider the well-known story of Adam and Eve. This story of two people placed in an ideal setting illustrates how human nature can undermine and compromise the quality of life.

Having been informed that a happy life would require a certain amount of self-discipline, Adam and Eve almost immediately proceeded to make a series of mistakes. The biggest mistake, however, was not in tasting the "forbidden" fruit. That was merely a result of curiosity, a God-given characteristic designed to stimulate our growth as human beings. You will always have curiosity, which means you will always be trying new things and testing your limits. That is normal, healthy and good for you.

The big mistake our "ancestors" made was in taking themselves too seriously once they realized they had overstepped their limits. If, instead of running and hiding in shame and fear, they had slapped their foreheads and exclaimed, "How stupid of us! What were we thinking?" they might have had a good laugh and you and I might still be living in a beautiful garden.

Unfortunately they overestimated their own importance, treated their mistake as an earth-shattering event, and sought to hide themselves from the painful realization that they were not equipped to be in charge. Hiding from the truth didn't work for them, and it still doesn't work for us today. Yet we continue to insist upon taking ourselves just as seriously as they did.

"Not me!" you're probably saying to yourself. "I love to laugh. I have a good sense of humor."

Well, step back in line. We *all* love to laugh, when it's the right time and the right place. Usually the right time is when you're "off the clock" or during your down time—when all your responsibilities have been met. Similarly the right place is a party or a theater—some kind of recreational setting. Put a responsibility or a challenge on your plate, however, and you immediately make the unfortunate and unhealthy decision to get serious.

And that's what's killing you.

Your seriousness is the basic underlying cause that is setting off your stress alarms with increasing frequency. Is it something dangerous? Can you do anything about it?

The answer is *yes* to both questions. The cause of your stress is, indeed, deadly dangerous, but there is a definitive and effective treatment available, an antidote that can stop today's stress epidemic in its tracks. You have this remedy within you. It has been there all along. It is your **humor nature,** or as you might better know it, your sense of humor.

You probably don't remember, but way back when you were only about six weeks old, you had a breakthrough moment. You made the first interpersonal communication of your life. You deliberately and consciously reached out to another human being for the first time.

Prior to this age, all your communications had been impersonal. You cried when you were wet and hungry; you cooed when you were warm and well fed. Any competent response from those around you could settle the issue. It wasn't personal.

However, by the time you reached six weeks, you had developed the capacity to focus your eyes sharply enough to recognize the familiar features of that face hovering over you and you had gained a measure of control over the movements of you little facial muscles.

It was at that momentous instant that you threw caution to the winds and attempted your first deliberate social encounter. Can you guess what you did? You smiled! That's right! It was not gas! It was a genuine smile.

When you put that smile on your face, you were saying "Hi!" for the very first time, before you had words or even thoughts, as we know them. It was you putting your best side forward, seeking welcome and approval from another person in what had to be a strange and sometimes scary world.

Who or what taught you to smile at that critical moment in your life?

No one taught you that smile, and no one had to. It was your natural inclination, your "hardwired" choice for putting your best foot forward. This is why I can say with assurance that you were born possessing a strong and vibrant natural humor nature.

You were not born with this deadly serious attitude about yourself. You learned that from the rest of us. The denigration of this healthy asset probably began in earnest when you started to attend school. There you met adults who were called teachers. Think back to how those adults in charge of your education responded when you brought those marvelous gifts of your smile and your playfulness with you to school.

"Wipe that smile off of your face!" "Get serious!" "So, you think that's funny, do you? I'll show you what's funny!" (I will always remember that last one, because they never did follow up on the promise to show me something funny.) These people were intent on teaching you and me that the best way to become a responsible and good person was to "get serious." Insidiously you learned that you had to be serious to be good.

The seed was planted.

In the years that followed, the process of your education and "maturation" into adulthood became a repetitious litany of the same lesson: Responsibility requires seriousness. You were a good student and you wanted to be responsible. So, you stifled your powerful humor nature in favor of seriousness in order to be successful. In time you came to regard humor as trivial and irresponsible, and you relegated this "best asset" to a very limited area of your life: the realm of entertainment and recreation.

And that's where things stand at present. Just like Adam and Eve you have learned to take yourself too seriously, and it fills every day of your adult life with stress and fear.

• FIND THE CURE •

All of this would be sad news indeed, if there were no effective remedy for your condition. Fortunately, as we have already noted, your **humor nature** exists within you, capable of eliminating your stress by treating its underlying cause: your seriousness.

That's right. Even though you have set it aside and tethered it tightly, your humor nature has never left you. It is just waiting for you to let it off its leash. Once you do, you will notice the many benefits of this natural healing power, benefits that have been documented by medical research.

In the last three decades there has been an explosion of scientific research into *humor's specific physical and mental effects.* We now have verifiable data confirming that a sense of humor improves your life in a host of ways.

1. HUMOR REDUCES STRESS

This is probably the easiest benefit to prove and is, of course, the central thesis of this book. If you laugh for 20 seconds, you double your heart rate, and it stays elevated for three to five minutes. When it comes back down, it temporarily goes lower than before the laughter. The same holds true for your blood pressure and your respirations. Pulse, blood pressure and respiratory rate are all commonly used to document the rise and fall of body tension. When all three go to a lower level, it usually means you have let go of stress.

It just so happens that this rising and falling pattern is the same way your body reacts to aerobic exercise. In laughter's case, however, you don't need special shoes or paraphernalia. You always have your workout equipment with you. Nor do you have to travel to a designated exercise place.

You might say that every minute you spend laughing is one less minute you would have to spend on the rowing machine or the Stairmaster. For me, that means I can experience aerobic benefits from my favorite piece of exercise equipment—the "Couch Master." I spend a lot of time on mine, but if I'm laughing, it's not wasted.

You see, laughter itself moves us from a state of higher physiologic tension to one of relatively lower tension. That is part of the reason why it feels so good. We enjoy letting go of tension. It brings release and relief. And get a load of this: The more often you laugh, the more long-lasting the relief.

One way to remind yourself about the practical stress-relieving potential of humor would be to consider your job stress. Most of us experience tension or stress at work from time to time. (If you don't, I want your job.) For many, work stress is constant.

Perhaps you have a boss or supervisor who puts pressure on you. (I certainly do, which is sad because I work for myself.) The next time you feel that kind of pressure from the boss, simply laugh in his or her face. In no time at all, your job stress, as well as your job, will be eliminated from your life. I told you it was simple.

Now, that is a joke! We both know it is a bad idea to laugh in the boss' face if you want to keep working there the next day. *So don't do that.* Wait until he or she walks away. Then, make a funny face or do something silly to release the tension that has built up in you. It won't affect your boss but it will affect you, and you'll feel better. (And you'll still have a job tomorrow.) A little silliness during life's most serious moments can greatly relieve stress.

Shortly after her mastectomy, breast cancer survivor Fran, her two teenaged daughters and her husband decided to go out for dinner. It was Fran's first social outing since her discharge from the hospital.

"How good is your chicken special?" Fran asked the waitress when it was her turn to order.

"Delicious," was the answer. "We have breasts, thighs and drumsticks and you get to choose two pieces in any combination."

"I'll take it," Fran said casting a mischievous look at both her daughters, "And I'd like two breasts, please."

The entire family burst out laughing, and the waitress is probably still wondering to this day what was so funny.

The best part of this story is that Fran was doing fine while relating this—and many other stress-reducing personal humor anecdotes—at a cancer recovery event held more than 15 years later.

Here's another piece of great news: It takes only an instant to receive laughter's stress-reducing benefits. It's like jumping into a cool mountain stream on a hot summer's day. You don't have to stay in very long to feel the refreshment. Your humor nature works very efficiently. Minutes of fun can dissipate the effects of hours of stress.

When laughter reduces your stress, it also lowers the levels of stress hormones circulating in your blood. Since these hormones usually suppress your immune response, having fewer of them in your bloodstream turns out to be a good thing for your immunity, which leads to the next reported humor benefit.

2. HUMOR BOOSTS IMMUNITY

"Laughter serves as a blocking agent," author Norman Cousins writes, "Like a bullet-proof vest, it may help protect you against the ravages of negative emotions that can assault you in disease."

The instant you begin to smile, your immune system gets stronger and more effective. Greater numbers of antibodies and immunity cells are released into your bloodstream. This is not a guarantee that you will never get sick. It just means you'll be more likely to have your best defenses available in case disease comes calling.

You see, an army of tiny blood cells called lymphocytes march around your body, patrolling the borders to keep undesirable elements out. Of course, you can't hear them marching because they don't wear boots. Actually they don't even have feet. *(Come on, work with me here!)* They're just little round white blood cells.

Come to think of it, they don't even march. They float. So I guess they'd be more like a Navy than an Army.

Anyway, this Navy/Army is made up of three units.

The first unit is the Watchdog Division. These little cells identify any "foreign" or unwanted intruders. Immediately—like Paul Revere—they alert the rest of the forces. They work a lot like the family dog when, as a teenager, you were trying to sneak in past curfew. You were careful not to make any noise, deftly stepping over all the squeaky floorboards. Suddenly, when you had just about made it to your room, man's best friend announced your homecoming to the entire neighborhood. "Hey everybody! Cliff's finally home!" The watchdog division would be real pests, except for one very important fact. They are on your side.

Next comes the Warrior Division. They are vicious little fighters with excellent memories. When the watchdogs sound the alarm, the warriors charge headlong into battle. They work together flawlessly to surround the intruder and destroy it. They are very aggressive killers. Once they meet an enemy they never forget its face. They can carry a grudge for generations. It's like getting on the wrong side of your mother-in-law. You never hear the end of it.

The third unit is the Peacemaker Division. These little guys blow the whistle when the battle has been won. Like the referee in a boxing match, they decide when enough is enough. They keep the warriors from going overboard and destroying normal structures and functions. When it's over, the peacemakers clean up the debris and restore normal balance and tranquility. The byword of this division is, "Why can't we all just get along?"

The point of this little tale is that, just as in the real military, when troops get overworked or fatigued, the battle plan may be compromised. The watchdogs fall asleep, the warriors forget, and the peacemakers lose their sense of balance. That all adds up to a less effective immune response, should your body be challenged.

Laughter is like "R and R" for your Navy/Army. Research confirms that with laughter all these divisions show up in larger numbers and do their jobs more efficiently. They become "all that they can be."

There is an experience quite commonly reported by performing comedians. Typically, it goes like this: The performer may have a scratchy throat or flu-like symptoms prior to a show. She decides to perform despite these conditions. As soon as she begins generating and communicating laughs, the symptoms disappear, and in some cases stay away for hours. Apparently laughter is at times able to mobilize impressive reinforcements for your Navy/Army.

3. HUMOR RELIEVES PAIN

In a famous passage from his best-selling book, *The Anatomy of an Illness*, Dr. Norman Cousins quantified the pain-relieving properties of humor during his protracted illness. "Ten minutes of a genuine belly laugh had an anesthetic effect and would give me at least two hours of pain-free sleep."

Steven, a 52-year-old man suffering from chronic, unremitting back pain, was reporting on a recent trip he had taken to visit his 10-week-old grandson.

"The first morning, I was sitting in the living room, having a second cup of coffee, when my daughter brought the little fellow in to see me. She asked if I wanted to hold him. She didn't have to ask twice.

"He was so small. It had been a long time since I'd held a baby in my arms.

"I was looking down at his sweet little face when he opened his eyes and looked directly back at me. Then he smiled. It was like the roof had opened up to let sunshine directly into the room. I felt a wonderful warm feeling all through me. I smiled back and we really connected.

"Then I noticed something. My pain was gone. The pain never leaves me, but, for just that moment, it disappeared completely. It was a miracle."

Humor doesn't actually relieve pain, but it raises your tolerance for pain, which amounts to the same thing. Even though this has been confirmed repeatedly, no one is sure why it happens.

It might be a result of the release of endorphins, which usually accompanies laughter, but no one has been able to prove it. Endorphins are chemicals manufactured by your body that can make you feel good...*really good!* (That's right. It turns out that your central nervous system produces better drugs than Central America. And, they're legal.)

The pain relief could also come from the release of muscle tension that occurs during laughter. When a certain part of the body hurts, the muscles in the painful region often tense up in an effort to protect the area from further pain. Paradoxically, this reaction usually makes the pain worse.

Laughter, on the other hand, relaxes muscles. The release can be dramatic (and as those with weaker bladders have discovered, sometimes embarrassing).

Or maybe the improvement just comes from the momentary distraction we get from a laugh. Anything that gets your mind off your pain, even if it's temporary, offers some relief.

Humor expert Allen Klein puts it this way: "Humor doesn't diminish pain—it makes the space around it get bigger." Whatever the mechanisms, the results are reliable and sometimes dramatic. If you have a painful condition, your humor nature offers you a deal—your pain may not be negotiable, but your degree of suffering certainly could be.

4. HUMOR DECREASES ANXIETY

We all know that allaying our anxiety is one of humor's most practical benefits. That is why most of the jokes you have heard in your lifetime address topics that are anxiety-provoking: God, sex, death, politics, etc.

As Oscar Wilde lay on his deathbed, for example, he reportedly pointed to some unattractive curtains on the window and said, "Either those drapes go, or I do."

Helen, a 37-year-old woman recovering from breast cancer, reported the following exchange she had with her oncologist during her chemotherapy.

"My hair had begun falling out in large clumps, and Dr. Franklin seemed more upset about it than I was. He was telling me not to worry, assuring me that it would grow back after the treatments. He even speculated that it might grow back curlier than before, as if that was going to make me feel better about it.

"Finally, I said to him, 'Don't sweat it, Doc. I look at it this way: I'm going to save a fortune on shampoo.'"

Humor is a handy way to master situations filled with anxiety. When you are less anxious you think more clearly and your memory is more reliable. You will have a more effective response to any challenge you are facing.

5. HUMOR STABILIZES MOOD

Laughter is often compared to the shock absorbers on a car. They don't take the bumps out of the road, but they do make the ride more comfortable.

There is a Yiddish proverb that says, "The smoothest way is full of stones." Inevitably, living involves physical and emotional "bumps and jolts," even in the best of times. If you will permit it, your humor nature will absorb most of these shocks and preserve a "smoother ride."

I was taking a walk around our farm early one summer morning, absorbing the peace and tranquility of the countryside. The air was cool. It was silent except for the awakening songs of the birds. The sun was about to appear on the horizon. Just as I was thinking how wonderful it was to have such a joyful experience, a deer fly landed on my neck and promptly bit me.

My immediate response was to laugh. I laughed at the audacity of the little critter to intrude into my "special" moment. I laughed at the realization that, no matter how "perfect" I try to make things, there is always a deer fly, or something like it, in the picture. I laughed at the absurdity of all that.

6. HUMOR RESTS THE BRAIN

Comedian Milton Berle described laughter as "an instant vacation." It turns out he's right. Fun is easier on the brain than fear and stress. Laughter actually gives the brain a rest. When you are laughing, the electrical activity of your brain is the same as when you are in a state of deep relaxation or meditation. (This is good news if you are someone who would like to enjoy the benefits of meditation without sitting still all that time.)

7. HUMOR ENHANCES COMMUNICATION

Perhaps the best example of humor as a communication enhancer is the frequent role assigned to laughter as an "ice-breaker" in social situations. Early in any encounter, humor reassures strangers that they have something in common, though it may not yet be identified. It is a powerful connection that can at times transcend language and culture to find a common ground we all inhabit.

Perhaps you have already discovered that, even in familiar relationships, humor can help you communicate things that are hard to talk about.

My friend Steven was near death. As a gynecologic surgeon, he had spent his entire professional life heroically "saving" women from the clutches of cancer. By some cruel irony of fate, he was succumbing, after a valiant personal struggle, to his own cancer.

I sat at his bedside in the hospital room, aware that this was likely to be the last time I saw him alive.

He opened his eyes and looked at me. I could tell he was glad to see me. He could tell I was grateful for a few quiet moments with him.

"Well, Steven," I said after I'd been there a while, "I've got to be going. I have to give a lecture to the second year medical students."

"Oh yeah? What are you going to lecture about?"

"The doctor-patient relationship," I answered. "If there's anything you would like me to say to them, I'd be happy to quote you."

"Yeah. Tell them first of all, they should always tell their patients the truth. And, second—never ask a patient to do something you're not willing to do yourself."

I broke out laughing.

"What are you laughing at?" he asked.

"Those are strange words coming from a male gynecologist, who has never had his feet in those stirrups."

He broke out laughing.

Steven died at home the next day. I will always be comforted by the memory of his laughter in our final conversation.

8. HUMOR INSPIRES CREATIVITY

Any interaction based on fun and endorsing laughter tends to lower inhibitions and stimulate spontaneity. That is a potent combination for creativity. At the same time humor usually introduces you to a new way of thinking about any subject. Often when you are laughing, you are acknowledging the discovery that certain things fit together in a new way.

For example:

An anxious mother calls the doctor, saying, "Doctor, come quickly. The baby just swallowed a ballpoint pen!"

The doctor replies, "I'm on my way. What are you doing in the meantime?"

The mother answers, "We're using a pencil."

If this joke brought a smile to your face, it's probably because the mother's absurd reply introduced you to a new way of understanding what the doctor meant when he asked, "What are you doing in the meantime?" You presumed, correctly, that the doctor was asking about the baby. The mother, however, thought he was asking about the pen. This little exercise in changing your perspective enabled you to "get the joke." The laughter is your incentive and, at the same time, your reward for creating a new understanding.

Another aspect of the humor experience that contributes to your creativity is that laughter and play lift you for brief moments out of any situation. Often the major impediment to your creative juices is the inability to "rise above" the confines of your present predicament to see the possibilities ahead.

One of my all-time favorite cartoons shows two prisoners hanging high on a dungeon wall, wrapped in chains from head to foot. One is turning to the other and whispering, "OK, here's the plan."

Cynthia, an attendee at a recent workshop, reported a game that had been popular in her family. She called it the "Progressive Story." One person would begin a story, using just one sentence: "Once upon a time, there lived a king who couldn't sleep at night." The next person had to add to the story, but was also confined to only one sentence.

In turn, everyone had a chance to move the story along, one sentence at a time. As the group played it, we noticed that the fun inspired lots of creativity. It became more and more difficult for players to confine themselves to just the one sentence. I could imagine this game turning into a marathon event.

9. HUMOR MAINTAINS HOPE

While a young seminary student was substituting for the church minister, the teenage daughter of a prominent church family was killed in an automobile accident.

The student minister went with fear and trepidation to the home of the stricken family, unsure of what he could do. The girl's father was in the living room, being comforted by friends and neighbors, but her mother was crying upstairs in her room.

The seminary student followed the pitiful wailing sound to the bedroom, where he found the mother lying on her bed with eyes closed, wailing out the pain of her broken heart.

He gently took her hand. The mother clung to his hand, but she neither opened her eyes, nor stopped wailing.

Squatting down beside the bed, the seminary student told himself it was important to maintain the human contact. After several minutes in the squatting position, however, his legs began to ache. He leaned back against what he thought was a closet door, but what turned out to be the bathroom door. It gave way and he suddenly fell backwards onto the woman's bathroom floor.

The wailing stopped. The woman sat up, opened her eyes, and burst into laughter. Then she stopped laughing abruptly, lay back down, closed her eyes and resumed her sobbing.

Mortified that he had failed mightily in his first attempt to be comforting, the seminary student left and continued to feel awful about his clumsy "faux pas."

Weeks later he was attending a farewell party given at the church on the eve of his departure, when the grieving mother approached him haltingly. "Thank you for what you did for me on the morning my daughter was killed."

"What was it that I did?" he asked cautiously.

"When you fell into our bathroom, you made me laugh," she said, "And the laughter gave me hope for the first time that I would get through the pain."

Laughter often offers promise during difficult moments, assurance that there will come a day when things will not be as bad as they seem.

"Laughter," the late great comedian Bob Hope said, "can transform almost unbearable tears into something bearable, even hopeful."

10. HUMOR BOLSTERS MORALE

Nowhere is humor a more essential morale boost than in the workplace—that powerful breeding ground for seriousness, and with it, stress. Shared humor enables competitive coworkers to laugh their way to common ground. It can create an enjoyable "time out" moment in the midst of pressure. Nothing raises comfort levels better than a well-placed laugh.

"You can turn painful situations around through laughter," comedian Bill Cosby says, "If you can find humor in anything, even poverty, you can survive it."

One morning, during our clinic staff meeting, I was reading out loud a letter I had received from a patient who was unhappy with the service I had provided during a recent appointment. As the clinic director, I thought it would be instructive for all of the staff to discuss the patient's complaints and brainstorm with me about how to improve my approach next time.

I reached a particularly angry sentence in the letter, which read, "Dr. Kuhn, let us suppose for a moment you are not God..." As I read this aloud, I sensed a sudden tension in the room. After all, I was the boss. How dare she address the chief in such sarcastic tones?

I looked up from the paper into the stunned faces of the residents, nurses and staff members sitting around the table.

Then I said, "OK—but only for a moment!"

The spontaneous laughter broke the tension and restored the faltering morale of the group.

HAPPINESS BLOCKERS

Humor is no "Johnny-come-lately" to the human arsenal. The Bible reports quite clearly in the book of Proverbs, "A happy heart is good medicine; and a cheerful mind works healing." And the annals of medicine are loaded with accounts of its healing power. Sir Thomas Sydenham, a 17th century physician of great note, wrote: "The arrival of a good clown is of more benefit to the health of a town than of twenty asses laden with drugs."

Voltaire, the French philosopher/playwright, was fond of saying, "The art of medicine consists of amusing the patient while nature cures the disease."

On the other hand, Abraham Lincoln was right on target when he mused, "People are usually about as happy *as they want to be*." As strange as it sounds, I have discovered that a lot of people don't want to be as happy as they think they do. Often it relates to the incessant indoctrination they have received throughout their lives on the high merits of seriousness. They feel irresponsible when they lighten up.

Others feel guilty for having a good time without having "earned" it by first living up to some idealized standard of perfection.

Then there are those who are afraid they might incur the jealousy and envy of others if they appear to be having too good a time.

The people who feel they have to keep things well in hand at all times make up by far the largest group of happiness avoiders. For them happiness and fun represent too much of a threat to decorum and control.

Some are afraid to let go of their emotional control.

Barbara, a middle-aged woman recovering from cancer had a reputation for "hiding" behind intellectualizations during support group meetings. When something humorous was shared, while others were laughing, she was more prone to analyzing why it was funny. She had been confronted about this many times and encouraged to get out of her head and into her heart; to become more spontaneous. Admitting that this was her way of controlling her emotions, she had asked the group to help her learn to loosen up.

During one session, she seemed to be getting somewhere. She was sharing her feelings in lieu of her thoughts. She was admitting her fears, instead of preaching intellectualized platitudes.

Hoping to support Barbara's efforts, another group member offered reinforcement.

"When I hear you share your feelings like that, I feel closer to you than at any other time. I hope you will continue to speak more from your heart instead of your head."

Without hesitation Barbara answered, "Thank you. I'm really going to think about that."

Everyone, including Barbara, laughed.

There are no easy answers to the kind of internalized perfectionism that insures you will never earn the right to have a good time. However, if you stick with the "HA HA HA Prescription" that is laid out in these pages, you will find that your humor nature will actually help you get out from under the tyranny of your uncompromising self-imposed standards. You will, for example, learn the difference between perfectionism and perfection, and recognize that one is possible, whereas the other never is.

And I will make you a promise. I will never ask or encourage you to do anything that will impair your self-esteem or the respect you seek from others who are important in your life.

To the people who are afraid of what others might think if they are seen having fun, I say: Get over it. It's time to stop being obsessed with the expectations of others. You're old enough to live your own life now. Besides, are you sure other people are paying that much attention to your life?

Finally, to those of you for whom having fun means losing that control over things that you value so highly, I have a special feeling for you, because I used to be one of you. I know how heavy a responsibility it is to always be the one who knows best how things should be. Do you know what I discovered? I was never as much in control as I thought I was. In retrospect, good outcomes that occurred on my watch happened as much in spite of me as because of me. Sometimes it's best to let things happen rather than make them happen.

The good news is you don't have to make fun happen. You just have to be willing to let it happen. Whenever you have the willingness, fun will materialize.

Step Two: Play to Win, Reject Victimhood

Our first grandbaby, Jordan, was fighting for his life in the "Preemie" ICU. He had been born six weeks early, underdeveloped and not breathing. Instead of being enfolded in his mother's welcoming arms, he was whisked into this special unit, surrounded by life-preserving machinery.

When Connie and I were allowed to visit him that first morning, you can imagine how much tension we were feeling. Our anxiety was made even worse by the presence of all the technology in the room—the blinking lights, the electronic alarms, all the huge machinery supporting such tiny, frail bodies. It was a daunting moment.

At that time we did not know what I will tell you now: We recently celebrated Jordan's twelfth birthday. He's a healthy and robust boy, full of energy and verve, the star of his Little League baseball team (at least his grandfather thinks so). But, we had no assurance of these things on that morning. We were, to say the least, uptight.

As we made our way to Jordan's incubator, Connie saw another baby under an ultraviolet light for control of jaundice.

She grabbed my arm and whispered, "What's that blue light?"

Without thinking, I just blurted out the first thing that came to mind. "Sweetheart, I think that baby's on sale for the next ten minutes."

Stupid? Absolutely!

Insensitive? I don't think so (It was heard only by the two of us).

Effective? You bet! When Connie jabbed me in the ribs with her elbow and whispered, "Cut that out," I knew that our tension had been broken and we were going to get through that experience a little more easily.

That, my friends, is the human *humor nature* in action; often not all that funny, but marvelously effective in getting us through tough challenges.

Less than a month after she learned the persistent pain in her right leg was a tumor called sarcoma, 15-year-old Darla sought my help. Her oncologist had told her she had only 18 months to live, but she informed me right off the bat that she was planning to go on much longer than a year and a half.

Darla had heard about some cancer patients who had been successful using relaxation and imagery to reinforce the effect of their chemotherapy treatments. She wanted to learn how to do that and she wanted to start immediately, if not sooner.

Our work together spanned more than five years until her death at age twenty. Those years were filled with many incredible moments for Darla—high school graduation, college, romance, marriage, a honeymoon in Hawaii and lots of laughter.

The most important lesson Darla taught me during those years was to laugh during serious moments. I had always "approved" of humor, but only in its place and time, which was after all responsibilities had been met. I was a serious doctor of medicine.

Darla maintained that if we adhered to my criteria, we might never laugh. She thought laughter's place was everywhere, and its time, any time.

Her sense of humor was audacious and spontaneous.

One day, after she had lost her hair from chemotherapy, Darla and her younger brother, Craig, were helping their mother hang curtains. Craig chauvinistically climbed the ladder. "You better let somebody strong do this," he told Darla.

"Oh yeah?" Darla retorted. "Well, I can do something you can't!"

"What's that?" Craig asked.

"This!" With that, Darla hooked her forefinger under her wig, lifted it off her head and began twirling it in the air.

As she recounted this to me in my office, she demonstrated the wig twirling. It was one of the funniest gestures I have ever seen. Her hairless scalp was shining, her eyes were sparkling and a triumphant grin beamed from her face.

We laughed together breathlessly for more than a minute.

It is an image I'll never forget.

• TRANSCENDENCE •

This is not an example of laughing away unwanted fears and burdens, making light of a painful experience. Rather it is an example of transcendence. Darla's cancer was very real and very serious. Instead of giving in to it, however, she chose to rise above the pain and fear.

Don't confuse what she did with avoidance. In avoidance, we ignore, deny or otherwise skirt an unwanted experience. In transcendence, we acknowledge that unwanted feeling or experience, but maintain a perspective that prevents those elements from disabling us.

Darla never shrank from confronting the harsh realities of her medical condition. Instead she chose to transcend them, to pack more living into her twenty years than most of us manage to do in four times that amount.

Darla's means of transcendence was understanding her *humor nature*—what it was and what it was for.

In a term paper written for her English Composition course during freshman year in college, Darla wrote:

> "... a sense of humor goes beyond the ability to tell an amusing anecdote and includes a capacity to see the positive aspects of otherwise adverse situations. I use my own sense of humor to help me remain sane through the difficult times in my battle with cancer."

How Darla figured this out at such a tender age, I do not know. All I can tell you is that she was a brilliant example of how humor sustains resilience. For all of us involved in her care, she became a "walking textbook" of *humor nature*. For me, she was—and still remains—an inspiration for the research I have pursued.

Her *humor nature* strategies are ones we could all benefit from employing because they are not restricted to those suffering from dire diseases. They are strategies that are useful in successfully alleviating the stress and angst of normal daily life:

—Don't waste time on self-pity. Instead of sitting around pondering "why me?" move on to the more important question "What's next?"

—Find the funny. Instead of assigning blame for your situation lighten its impact by taking note of some of life's ironic twists, its amusing incongruities.

—Understand the difference between acceptance and approval. Darla never approved of her cancer, but she accepted it as her personal challenge, almost from day one of her diagnosis.

• EXPECTATIONS AND ENTITLEMENT •

I see fewer and fewer of Darla's traits in our society today. We seem to have lost our ability to accept the challenges of dealing with the unexpected and unwanted elements of our lives, preferring instead to expend our efforts in finding something or someone to blame.

My year of internship was the most physically taxing year of my life. For several months my schedule required me to be on duty for 36 hours, then off only 12. Every other night was spent at the hospital. On the "easy" rotations, I only had to work every third night. Even though it's forever etched in my memory, the whole year seems like a blur of constant exhaustion.

When I began my residency and discovered that I was required to be on duty only every fifth or sixth night, I thought I had died and gone to Nirvana. I actually was able to have a life away from the hospital. Then in the third month of the first year the spell was broken. I was assigned to work every fourth night. I remember feeling abused and exploited. How dare they mistreat me that way? I complained bitterly to my chief, who simply pointed out that three months earlier I would have been grateful for such a "soft" schedule.

He was right. I was amazed at how quickly I had become acclimated to the lighter demands on my time. It had only taken me two months to feel abused by a workload I would have gladly welcomed at the beginning. In eight short weeks I had grown to feel *entitled* to my new quality of life.

I bring this up because it illustrates how quickly we can raise the standards of what is acceptable and claim "entitlement" to new levels of comfort. Despite having done nothing to earn it, all of us seem to feel we have a right to a quality of life that would have been considered excessively luxurious a generation ago. And the oncoming generation appears to expect more of everything, in half the time, with half the effort.

How did we get this way? I think it's an inevitable byproduct of the high aspirations upon which our country was founded. Guaranteeing life, liberty and the pursuit of happiness to everyone is indeed a lofty and ambitious game plan. This is not to disparage the vision. Overall, I think the results speak for themselves. Despite our inconsistencies and imperfections, it's clear that we've come closer to achieving those near impossible goals than any other nation in history.

However there's a downside to creating such high expectations. It is easy to misconstrue the guarantee of *an opportunity to freely pursue* happiness, and regard it as a guarantee of happiness itself. By virtue of their citizenship, people are quick to feel it is their birthright to be happy. Thus expectations are raised that cannot be fulfilled. When it doesn't happen as "promised," folks feel disillusioned and victimized.

The proof is all around us. We've become a nation of victims. Everybody blames his or her plight on something or someone else. And, we want compensation for our "victim" status. This has represented a windfall for the legal profession. Only rarely do we see someone willing to take personal responsibility for his problems. Passing the buck has become our national pastime.

It has now even seeped into our language. We read about a person being "hit by a car," when, in fact, he was hit by another person who was driving a car. Cars don't run into things. People do. We should have seen this coming with the advent of "no fault" insurance.

I think this spirit of "I'm not to blame" is just one more example of our taking ourselves too seriously. I call it the DBM (Don't Blame Me) mentality—or, for those more inclined to diagnostics, **inflammatory victimitis**. Are you a "victim" of this mentality? Here are some ways to tell. If you can answer "yes" to any of these questions, you may be suffering from victimitis:

"VICTIMITIS": A SELF-TEST

—Have you ever caught yourself just waiting around for your talents to be "discovered?"

—Do you think that weighing 500 pounds and eating every meal at the donut castle is just coincidental?

—Do you consider your most recent DUI an instance of bad luck?

—Do you ever envy handicapped people for getting all the good parking spots?

—Have you complained about your poor luck with the lottery, but never bought a ticket?

—Do you scold your dog every time you fart?

—When your team loses, do you always attribute it to poor officiating?

—Have you ever spilled hot coffee on yourself and thought about suing somebody?

—When your kid brings home a bad grade, do you usually blame the teacher?

—Have you ever considered your tooth decay to be the result of global warming?

Although it pains me to admit it, the men in our society might just be a little more susceptible to a victimitis mentality than the women. In the midst of writing this section, I took a break to feed my goldfish in our backyard pond. When I couldn't find the fish food on the shelf I expected it to be on, I immediately asked my wife, "Where did you put the goldfish food?"

Then I "found" the jar, on the next shelf down, exactly where I had placed it the evening before.

My wife chuckled. "I hope you're including that in your book," she said.

I would estimate that 99% of all men experience an acute onset of victimitis (i.e. automatic accusation of their spouses of tampering) when they can't find something. The other 1% live alone.

And while we're on the subject, I am not only guilty of practicing victimitis as a husband; I am also guilty of instilling it as a psychiatrist. By advancing the notion that early life experiences and relationships can be responsible for current behavior, my colleagues and I have subtly encouraged a victim mentality. (Recently I remarked to one of my patients, "You seem to have great difficulty taking personal responsibility for anything." "Yeah!" he replied swiftly, "I get that from my mother.")

If I've contributed in any way to your victimitis, I want to make at least partial amends right now. Therefore, if you had to honestly answer yes to any of the questions in the previous list, let me offer you a technique that has proved helpful for many of my patients caught in the same trap. What you may need is to be "shocked" out of the certainty that you are a victim, and nothing does that better than challenging yourself with a well-placed question that will open up alternative possibilities.

For example, recently one of my patients was going on and

on about his limitations, all of which he seemed convinced were attributable to his father.

"I'm a loser because my father was a heavy drinker," he concluded with an elongated sigh.

All I did was ask a quiet simple question, using his very own terminology.

"Could it be that your father drank so much because he saw you were such a loser?"

Not an easy thing to say. Not an easy thing to hear. He has yet to thank me for the effort. Maybe he never will. He hasn't asked for another appointment yet, but that may not be a bad thing. If he was "shocked" into taking more personal responsibility, he may have discovered he didn't need a psychiatrist's help.

I'm not suggesting you be flippant. I'm just saying that whenever you find yourself assessing a situation as all one way, try considering the possibility that it might be just the opposite. If it looks all white, maybe it's really all black? If you think its all their fault, what if it was all yours? When you do this for yourself, I predict you'll discover that the truth lies somewhere in the middle. It may take a while to nail it down, but in the meantime, at least you have escaped the extreme victim mindset. You have begun to seek your part in the situation.

• WANTS AND NEEDS •

Nowadays, most people seem to think the word freedom means "free ride." This probably isn't a new phenomenon. However, it's a misperception tinged with real irony, because the opposite is much closer to the truth. The more freedom we have, the more personal responsibility we must assume. Will Rogers must have seen something like this decades ago, when he suggested that we needed to balance the east coast's Statue of Liberty with a Statue of Responsibility on the west coast.

The blind alley this misperception leads you into can be described as follows. First, an unrealistic sense of entitlement leads to unrealistic expectations. Once this process begins, it is human nature to continue upping the ante of expectations. Satisfaction seems to last only as long as someone fails to imagine something better. Inevitably the exceptional becomes merely the expected. It's as if Americans are looking unprecedented prosperity right in the face and shouting with one voice, "What have you done for me lately?"

Here are some examples to back up my case:

In the 1990s, Americans investing in the stock market held onto their shares an average of 24 months. Stockholders have become so impatient today that the average holding time is down to one year.

Although it has been documented that American consumer products today are lower priced and higher quality than products on the market a decade ago, the American Customer Satisfaction Index has gone down steadily over the last ten years.

Our impatience seems to have no limits. Comedian Steven Wright quips, "Yesterday I made instant coffee in my microwave and actually went backward in time."

Unrealistic and unconstrained expectations tend to race ahead of the ability to fulfill them. Frustration, exhaustion and disillusionment are the results. Over time, this builds to resentment and a sense of being victimized. Living life with a victim mentality is not only an unhealthy perspective, but also one that absolutely insures less than optimal success and happiness. Quite frankly, it perpetuates and multiplies your symptoms of stress.

Francine's friend, Celia, has just had her kitchen redone—the latest quartz counter tops, fancy imported tile backsplashes, all the most updated appliances. Is Francine happy for Celia? Not at all. Francine is dying of jealousy.

Not that Francine's kitchen is anything to sneer at. It is spacious and attractive, with lots of natural light pouring through large windows. In fact, she actually bought her current home just a few years back *because* of the kitchen. However, now that she has seen Celia's new one, Francine can no longer be happy with what she has. She is instead preoccupied and frustrated by what she doesn't have.

Your frustrated sense of entitlement encourages you to remain preoccupied with all the things you want that you do not have. If you look around you, you'll notice that modern culture reinforces this preoccupation. Notice how frequently the words "I want" can be heard in the commercials on television. When you become so focused on what you want, you become insensitive to what you really need. Worse yet, you may fall into the trap of assuming your wants and your needs are the same. You literally think you need everything you want.

Once you are in this mental trap, you can't win. It's like trying to fill a leaky bucket. The only way out is to learn to separate your wants from your needs. When you can do this you will find that your needs can be met, whereas your wants are never completely satisfied. Thus, your health and success depend upon your ability to operate on the basis of your needs, not your wants. Here are some guidelines that will help you distinguish between your needs and wants:

—Your needs are always smaller than your wants.

—Your wants always cost more in time and money than your needs.

—There is a difference between satisfaction and satiation.

—Satisfaction meets your needs. Satiation extinguishes your wants, and then only for a little while, after which they come back even stronger.

—Your needs involve very little emotion. If you find yourself full of emotion, chances are you are chasing your wants.

—Your needs seldom change. Your wants change often and with relatively little provocation.

—Fulfilling your needs brings serenity and prosperity. Fulfilling your wants leads to addiction.

—Wants are represented by obsessive thoughts and compulsive cravings. Needs are represented by a deep commitment to healthy development.

—Fulfilling your wants ultimately requires taking from others. Meeting your needs helps others, because it involves encouraging others to meet theirs.

—Your ego drives your wants. Your humor nature advocates for your needs.

In the steps to come you are going to learn how to utilize these characteristics to attain a higher quality of life and truer happiness. It is enough for now that you recognize that being driven by your wants will consign you to lifelong frustration, because you will never get them fulfilled. And you know what? That's just as well, because getting what you want will never provide the joy, happiness and success you seek. Those things, as well as the stress-free health you yearn for, are assured as soon as you get what you need.

Recognizing the difference between wants and needs is the first step toward leaving your victim mentality behind forever, as Darla was able to do. **You will never get everything you want, but you will always get everything you need—even if you don't want it.** How do I know? Listening to countless personal stories like this one that follows has opened my eyes.

As she was leaving a Chicago hotel after giving a speech at a corporate conference, Judy noticed there was an elevated train station right across the street. Since the elevated went directly to the airport, and since it was not likely to be crowded on a Sunday afternoon, she decided to take the train instead of a taxi.

Judy proceeded to the gate, inserted her token, and pushed her oversized suitcase ahead of her through the turnstile. Halfway through, her luggage got wedged under the front turnstile arm, and the other arm of the turnstile had come up behind her. Judy couldn't budge. When she tried to back up, she discovered those gates only go in one direction. There was no reverse.

So there Judy was—trapped like a bird in a cage in a totally deserted station watching helplessly as her train to the airport came, stopped, opened its doors, and, when no one got off and no one got on, closed its doors and left.

Judy was frustrated, embarrassed, angry, and a little bit scared. The possibility of missing her plane was beginning to dawn on her. She began to wonder how long it might be before any one would find her. Her family wasn't even expecting her back home until early evening. It might take them hours to organize a search party from 500 miles away.

"Could you use some help?" Judy looked up to find a man in a transit uniform standing before her on the platform. A dream come true.

"I am really stuck," she answered sheepishly.

"See if you can climb out over the back railing," he suggested. "I'll try to pull your bag through."

It worked. The only problem was the turnstile clicked. So, now Judy and her luggage were both free, but on opposite sides of the gate.

"Don't worry," the man reassured her, signaling a colleague down the platform, "We'll get you another token."

"I don't know what I would have done if you hadn't come along," Judy told him as they waited. "I already missed one train. Now, thanks to you, I might still make my flight."

He frowned. "Where are you heading?"

"Midway Airport."

The man looked at Judy with pure pity in his eyes. "Miss, you're on the wrong side of the tracks for the airport train."

This doesn't demonstrate an understanding on Judy's part about her needs versus her wants, because at the time, she confesses, she wasn't aware of any distinction between the two. But, it's a great example of how her eyes became opened to the difference. That afternoon, fate awakened Judy to the recognition that, although she certainly didn't want to get stuck in that turnstile, if she was to have any chance of getting home that night, she needed to be prevented from getting on the wrong train. Fate sometimes has a way of doing for us what we can't do for ourselves. Perhaps you've had an experience similar to Judy's. Of course, whenever that occurs, the trick is to pay attention to the lesson.

For my part, once my eyes were opened to the difference between my own needs and wants, it became possible to more readily recognize the value of regarding them as separate categories. And this has led me over the years to develop strategies for keeping the distinction clearly in focus. We will examine some specific strategies for this when we get to Step Four, but the following example will demonstrate the practical value of remembering to differentiate between wants and needs.

In Frank Capra's perennially popular film, *It's A Wonderful Life*, there's a scene in which a panicked crowd of customers storms the Savings and Loan building with the intention of withdrawing all of their money. Jimmy Stewart's character, realizing that there is not enough cash in the till to satisfy all the demands, comes up with a plan to save the financial integrity of the institution.

He explains that most of the money is not on the premises, since it has been invested in various mortgages and loans. He asks each person in line to modify his cash demands down to only what he will need for the next day or two. He predicts that if every member will be satisfied with only what she needs, instead of what she wants, they will get through the crisis together, and the Savings and Loan will not have to go out of business.

It takes some cajoling and encouragement, but gradually each member accepts only the money for his immediate needs and leaves the rest. In case you are among the very few people left on earth who have not seen this film, I'll tell you that they make it through the business day with one dollar to spare.

The lesson here is clear. If we become willing to accept only what we need, ignoring what we want, sufficient resources will always be available. Needs can be met. Desires are bottomless pits.

We are now really talking about the difference between expectation and hope. Your expectations are rooted in your wants and desires. Hope relates more to your needs. Therefore, hope is never groundless because your needs can be met. On the other hand, expectations are bound to be forever frustrated, simply because you will never get everything you want. With this in mind, a sensible approach might be to keep your hopes high and your expectations low.

Therefore, as ridiculous as it sounds, instead of feeling like a victim when you experience frustrated desire, I think you should be grateful. Not getting what you want is your cue to refocus on your needs and thereby your hope.

The key discipline here is not that of squelching all desire. Even if you could do that—which you can't (so don't try)—life would be pretty dull and tedious. Instead, I suggest you work on bringing your desires into line with your needs. In other words, practice wanting only what you need.

A young couple I know very well would probably be the poster family for "minimalism." Their home is furnished adequately, but sparsely by today's standards. They do not collect "things" and are especially resistant to gadgetry. Before they purchase an appliance, they have long discussions, pro and con, and do lots of comparison-shopping. Clothing purchases for them and their children are similarly analyzed beforehand, and they have a rule that, unless there is a specific need for the new article, nothing new can be added to the closet unless something old is discarded. To say that they were disciplined in this regard would be an understatement.

It's hard to ignore the results. When you visit their home, you find a living area that is open and spacious, uncluttered by the kind of paraphernalia most of us tend to accumulate. Their kids have more room to play and the adults never feel cooped up. Because they have fewer things to distract them, they have more time to spend with each other. Not a bad trade-off—less things, more time.

Your humor nature can help you here. It can make anything more fun for you, even the things you don't want. In this way, meeting needs can be more appealing. You can actually come to want something you need without liking it at all. I know that sounds ludicrous, but it works.

Here's an example.

Frank, a salesman, is on the road most of the time. Here is how he has learned to handle a tedious part of his schedule.

"When I travel, the bane of my existence is calling in for my voicemail messages every day. It helps if I make a game out of it. I keep a log of the time it takes from the first dialed number to the hang-up at the end.

I try to beat my record for brevity, which now stands at 25 seconds. If there are a lot of messages, I have a backup plan. I go for the longest time. My current marathon record is 14 minutes and 37 seconds. Whenever I can beat either of these marks, I treat myself to a movie or a ballgame.

It makes it more fun to call in, and either way I have something to shoot for."

Why not let your humor nature help you make the things you need to do more appealing by turning them into "games" you can look forward to? You will find that, although you remain a "victim" of circumstances, it doesn't matter, because you can always be a "master" of response. It is only a matter of adjusting your attitude.

A friend of mine plays a "game" with herself whenever she is contemplating a major purchase personally or for her family. She periodically "visits" the thing she's thinking of buying. She actually goes to the store regularly and spends time with the merchandise, sometimes extending the process over months or even years. She says this helps her really get to know the ins and outs of the product.

It's also fun, because she assumes a kind of thrill of "ownership," without ever risking the purchase price. This often staves off her need to buy the object. It sometimes happens that, either she outgrows her enthusiasm for the product, or it goes out of style before she ever makes the purchase.

Using their humor natures, Frank managed to make a tedious task more enjoyable, and my friend greatly enhanced the pleasure of making (or not making) a consumer purchase. Neither could control the situation. What they could control, however, was *their attitudes*, the way they permitted their situations to affect them. We can all do that.

Let's go back for a minute to my stint as a 25-year-old medical intern, working 36 hours on and 12 hours off.

I was losing my mind from lack of sleep, job pressure, and not being home to help my young wife take care of our screaming infant son.

"I don't know if I can make this work," I complained to my mentor one evening, "I'm beginning to hate this job."

"Well, Cliff," she replied, "how is that attitude working for you?"

"What do you mean?" I shot back. "Look at my life! Are you suggesting that I'm responsible for my situation?"

"You're not responsible for your situation," my mentor calmly answered, as she refilled her coffee cup, "But you are responsible for your frustration."

You, too, may be as hesitant to accept control of your attitudes as I was. You may occasionally feel more comfortable playing the role of the victim, pretending that your attitudes are an uncontrollable byproduct of your environment and circumstances. The good news is ... nothing could be further from the truth.

Here are five questions to ask when you feel out of control. Each will place the reins of your attitudes squarely back in your own hands:

—*What is there in my life that I can be grateful for and how can I express that gratitude right now?*

—*How have I improved since the last time I addressed this challenge?*

—*What should my next step be?*

—*How will any of this look a year from now? 10 years? 100 years?*

—*I know what I want, but what do I really need from this situation?*

• FUN AND FEAR •

How can you motivate yourself to do those things you need to do? You essentially have only two choices: fun or fear. You either do something because you enjoy it or you do it because you're afraid not to. Either can be a very powerful "fuel" for your behavior.

If you're like most of us, fear is a frequent and reliable motivator. In fact, it may be your most frequent "fuel." Why do you stop at a STOP sign? What motivates you to observe the speed limit? Why do you pay your income taxes? What stops you from giving your boss a piece of your mind? A lot of what you do is motivated by the fear of the consequences that could result from *not* doing it.

And fear is indeed powerful, isn't it? It is capable of stimulating extraordinary levels of achievement. A truck bearing down on you can "inspire" you to get out of its way promptly and efficiently. A mother in a moment of fear may find the strength to lift an automobile off of her child who is trapped underneath it. Crafty leaders use fear tactics to manipulate followers into a state of compliance with their demands.

Fear-inspired responses are at times literally life saving. There is, however, a limitation built into the choice of fear as a constant or even frequent "fuel."

Fear is a hot burning fuel. By that I mean it consumes a lot of energy. Why? Because it is not your natural fuel. Just as you were not born serious, you were not born afraid. You had to be taught to be afraid. It required constant reinforcement, and still does.

Therefore, when you choose fear as the fuel for your behavior, it takes a constant effort to keep the fear alive, once the initiating moment is passed. Eventually this drains precious energy from you, energy that could otherwise be devoted to accomplishing your lofty objectives. In time this energy drain will cause you to either compromise your goals or become ripe for "burnout." (Imagine what would become of that mother if she decided she had to lift that automobile off the ground every day.)

By definition, if fear is your motivation, you are playing not to lose. Have you ever watched a sports team that is "playing not to lose?" Often toward the end of a basketball game one team, on the assumption it has scored enough points to win, will slow the pace of the game in hopes that the clock will run out before the other team can catch up. It's called "sitting" on the lead.

The team that adopts this "stalling" tactic changes its energy and chemistry immediately. Before the slow-down, its players were spontaneous, aggressive and energetic. After the shift, they become tentative, conservative clock-watchers. The winning momentum has disappeared. It is no longer much fun to watch this team, because all the fluidity of execution is gone. Unwittingly, these players have actually increased their chances of losing, because, if they have miscalculated and the other team catches back up, it is unlikely they will be able to recapture their previous momentum. These are the characteristics you have whenever you find yourself "playing not to lose."

So, despite its spectacular potential in the short run, fear turns out to be an inefficient fuel choice for the long haul. Since the success and good health you seek requires more of a marathon than a sprint, you would be wise to choose a better fuel for your journey.

Fun is the only other choice available to you, but it is a great one. With fun, you draw on positive energy and motivation. No longer are you driven to avoid unwanted consequences. Instead you are attracted to and motivated by the pleasure and satisfaction of doing the right thing. Fun is a far better choice than fear for several reasons.

Fun is your natural fuel. As you have already learned, you were born knowing how to play. No one had to teach it to you.

This afternoon I observed Joey, a two year old, playing at a local playground. He was the youngest child in the group, which also included his seven-year-old brother, William. It was impossible for me to figure out what kind of game they were playing, but one thing was very clear. Joey was involved.

He couldn't run as fast or jump as high as the others. He didn't have the vocabulary to successfully communicate verbally. Nevertheless, these "shortcomings" did not get in the way of his having as much fun as any child in the group.

Joey just ran and laughed, climbed over obstacles, and then ran and laughed some more. The other kids seemed to be enjoying his participation as well. They integrated him completely into what looked to me like senseless play. There was nothing Joey had to do to qualify. Like any toddler, he was born to have fun.

Because it is so natural to you, *fun requires much less effort than fear.* It's the difference between paddling a canoe with the current or against it. When you are going with the current you are in the natural flow and this actually adds to the energy available to you. So it is with fun.

Not only will you conserve personal energy, but also *the positive flow of fun will compound your resources.* Soon two plus two may actually equal five instead of four. Your energy will go farther and last longer. The limits you have learned to place on your effectiveness can easily disappear, as you let go of fear and let your humor nature carry you along.

Smiling is one of the most effective ways to release the power of your humor nature. Veteran joggers often report a kind of "high" that can result from the decision to simply and deliberately smile when fatigue or pain threaten to undermine their resolve to continue running.

I have tried this technique myself and can attest to its effectiveness. The simple act of forcing a smile on my face, while continuing to run, usually results in a noticeable surge of energy and at least a temporary easement of pain and discomfort.

Besides this exponential economy of energy, there is another reason you can expect your effort to be more sustainable when fun is your "fuel." *Fun is psychologically more appealing than fear.* Gaining a positive is going to be more desirable to you over time than just escaping a negative. Avoiding a loss is not the same as winning.

When it came to the clinical usefulness of hypnosis for cessation of smoking, renowned medical hypnotist Dr. Herbert Speigel found thirty years ago that a patient had a better chance of success if offered a post hypnotic suggestion that focused on the *positive* effects of not smoking, rather than the negative effects of continuing the habit.

At the time, it was common for anti-smoking hypnosis protocols to include an aversion motif, usually consisting of a suggestion that the taste of a cigarette would become extremely noxious to the smoker—something to be avoided. Most of the patients who were subjected to this approach, stopped smoking temporarily, and then returned to the habit in a matter of months.

Spiegel reported more encouraging results from an enhancement motif, in which the patient was given suggestions that focused on the optimum health of his body when unencumbered by the effects of smoking. Patients in this category were able to interrupt their smoking habits as successfully as those in the first group. The difference was that a higher percentage of them went on to sustain their freedom from the habit for a longer period of time.

Think of a sports team you have watched that was playing to win. It was exciting. The players were spontaneous and aggressive. There was abundant spirit and enthusiasm. And, when the buzzer signified the game's end, you saw a further explosion of energy in the celebration. Compare that to the "sigh" of relief at game's end, so characteristic of the team playing not to lose.

Both fun and fear are effective motivators in the short run, but only fun will provide lasting, sustainable results.

My son and collaborator, Greg, told me of his own recent firsthand experience of using fun, rather than fear, to motivate people in a tough situation.

"Manual High School in Louisville, Kentucky enjoyed the unique position of having the top scores in the entire state, as well as being ranked one of the nation's top high schools by Redbook Magazine. Yet by state mandate, Manual was required to continue improving its scores every year or risk being declared 'a school in decline.'

A school in decline? You can imagine the stress that threat created for Manual's administration and teaching staff. Teachers spent every professional development opportunity learning skills to help their students do well on the state tests, and soon the pressure trickled down to the students. The kids knew how important the test was and how much their teachers were stressing it.

Knowing that success rarely results when stress (or fear) is the motivating force, I racked my brain for a way to inject some fun-based motivation. In a speech to the Manual Junior class a week before the test, it suddenly came to me. I told them if they surpassed last year's state test scores, I, their assistant principal, would willingly make a fool of myself and ... break-dance for them.

The students went wild, jumping and cheering. Throughout the week, and during the week of testing, students were telling me that they were working hard so that they could see me break-dance. And guess what happened? Not only did Manual high school beat the previous year's score, but we also did it by a whopping four points!

Did I break-dance for the students? Of course! Did my offer to break-dance cause Manual's students to perform that well on the state tests? Maybe. But I know that it gave them a fun-based motivation to shoot for amidst all the stress and fear-based motivation of not letting the school down.

Another great example of the dramatic difference between fun and fear as potential "fuel" was in evidence during the 2002 Winter Olympics held in Salt Lake City. On the night of the final competition for women's figure skating, there were four women in contention—and, of course, only three medals. Since teenager Sarah Hughes from Baltimore, Maryland was in fourth place, she was out of the medal competition.

In an interview before the event, Miss Hughes said, "I realize

I have nothing to lose. So, I'm just going to skate my best and have fun tonight."

Well, the youngster from Baltimore executed her game plan to near perfection. Her routine was essentially flawless, but what I will never forget was the expression on her face when she finished. She was absolutely ecstatic with joy, flushed with the knowledge that she had done her very best. At that particular moment the issue of a medal appeared to be eclipsed by the deep satisfaction she felt.

The other three skaters each had something to lose and skated accordingly. They were fearful, tentative and conservative in their routines. Uncharacteristically, each one fell at least once during her performance. Skating not to lose, they fell short of their full capabilities. We shouldn't be surprised. Fun will always outperform fear. It never fails. Sometimes it happens quickly and dramatically; sometimes slowly and subtly. Chalk up yet another reason to upgrade your attitude toward one of more respect for and trust of your humor nature.

Here's one more detail about your choice of fun over fear: There is no middle ground between these choices, because one cancels out the other. They do not coexist. There is no fun in fear; and fun is essentially fearless.

I hope by now you are beginning to see that fun deserves at least as much, if not more, of your respect and trust as you have been giving to fear. Should you need even more reasons to upgrade your humor attitude, let me introduce you to Step 3.

Step Three: Choose Fun Over Funny

My parents always wanted me to be a doctor—a *real* doctor like a family physician or a surgeon. When I announced my decision to become a psychiatrist, my father was barely able to conceal his disappointment. "Son," he blurted out, "are you trying to be funny?"

(Neither of us realized at the time just how prophetic his question was.)

I was definitely not trying to be funny. On the contrary, I became a very serious practitioner of medicine in general, and psychiatry in particular.

My patients began showing me, practically from day one, however, that humor was a valid and valuable resource for healing. There was spontaneous humor in psychotherapy sessions, healing laughter between a married pair whose physical relationship had been "challenged" by the husband's spinal cord injury, and many cancer patients using humor to survive. It took a while to sink in, but when it did, I wanted to learn as much as I could about humor's healing powers.

How could I as a doctor help a patient restore a lost sense of humor and sustain laughter in the face of illness? How could I bring more humor to each "bedside" in a responsible, yet effective, way?

The answers to these questions were not in my medical books, so I sought the advice of "specialists" in a different field. I sought out comedians, who urged me not only to go to comedy clubs and listen, but to try performing in them too. It was their contention that the very best place to learn the techniques and mechanisms of human laughter was up on stage in front of an audience.

I learned something else along the way: fear.

Imagine yourself stark naked, exposed by a glaring spotlight, in front of 250 silent, unseen strangers staring up at you from the darkness. This gives you some idea of how I felt, as I walked (fully clothed) with uncertain steps to the center of a small stage. Apprehension constricted my throat. Sweat began trickling down my back (that spotlight is hot!) and a hollow sensation settled into my stomach.

In thirty years of practicing medicine, I had experienced my share of fear—fear that I might not be able to find the right words to comfort a family whose member had died without warning, or ease the rage of a husband, helpless over his wife's terminal disease, or assure a community disrupted by the outrageous behavior of a mentally ill neighbor. At such moments, there had always been a fleeting desire to be elsewhere.

But this was very, very different. Instead of answers to their questions, these anonymous, invisible people wanted laughter. They expected me to be funny. The biggest lesson I learned from this experience is the one I'm sharing with you in Step 3.

I had been performing standup for almost a week with Jim, a seasoned veteran of the comedy club circuit. "Cliff, " Jim asked one night, during dinner, "Do you mind if I ask you a personal question?"

"Of course not," I responded. "What's on your mind?"

"I was just wondering," he said. "Have you ever tried telling the truth up on stage?"

"I don't understand."

"I notice you tell an awful lot of lies in your act," he continued. "You say things about yourself that I can see aren't true, now that I've gotten to know you."

"But Jim, they're jokes! You know, set ups for punch lines. The idea is to make them laugh. Right?"

"I guess I assumed you would have noticed by now the difference between making them laugh and sharing a laugh with them," he continued.

"That's an interesting distinction," I said. I wanted to hear more.

He lit a cigarette. "To me, performing comedy is a lot like a sexual relationship, in that, if two people having sex are technically knowledgeable and competent, if they both know the right buttons to push, it can be extremely pleasurable. But that's nothing compared to the intensity that results when they make love. I think when you're making the audience laugh, your having sex with them. But if you're sharing a laugh with them, you're making love. And you can feel the difference in the interaction."

"Interesting analogy," I mused.

"I've watched you all this week. You're working too hard at it, son. *(I loved it when he called me son. At that point in my comedy career, he was the only comedian I had worked with who was older than I.)* The effort shows when it's supposed to look effortless. You're not having any fun and, when you don't have fun, the audience doesn't have fun either. Cliff, it's really more important to have fun on stage than to be funny."

It is the most profound insight any comedian has ever given me. For the rest of the week, he was at my shoulder before every performance, and just as I was ready to step out onto the stage each night, he would whisper, "Have fun out there."

I quickly began to experience a change. Focusing on fun led me to adopt three new performance "rules."

#1: Find Common Ground

My relationship with the audience became less adversarial. If they were there to have fun, and I shared the same goal for myself, there was no need to "win them over." All we had to do was find the things we both enjoyed talking about.

#2: Be Playful

I became more spontaneous in my delivery. If fun was now more important than funny, I could be playful, even when a joke "bombed." This immediately reduced the performance anxiety I had been feeling.

#3: Share The Spotlight

The more I embraced fun and "forgot" funny, the more I was able to allow audience members to play a bigger role in the performance. It became more of a "two-way street," whereas before the full responsibility was solely on my shoulders.

Using these rules, I relaxed enough to have fun with the audience, and the quality of the laughter changed. It became more spontaneous and energetic compared to the relatively more strained and hesitant laughs I was getting before. It's a difference that can be heard from the stage. It's almost palpable.

When I was trying to "make them laugh," the laughter had felt like a measure of approval (thumbs up or thumbs down). When I focused more on having fun and "sharing my fun with them," the laughter felt more like a measure of gratitude. There was less tension in the air. The audience started responding *with* me instead of *to* me. After my performances, I was hearing "Thank you" from audience members, when previously I had heard "Good job."

Most important, as I got better at the distinction between fun and funny, my performances became more personal. I stopped trying to be clever or witty just to get a laugh and began sharing my point of view—"here's what confuses me, here's what frustrates me, and here's what makes me laugh." I soon eliminated material that did not reflect my viewpoint, no matter how witty or clever it was. As the need to be "someone I wasn't" dropped away, I was able to be more comfortable in my own skin on stage. My rising comfort level produced a parallel rise in the audience's.

Thus, concentrating on fun delivered me from the desperate pressure of fear, which had previously dominated my performances. I wish I could tell you that it went away completely, but I won't lie. However, I can report continuing progress on that score to this day. Fun will deliver you from your fears as well, but first, you have to know how to tell the difference between fun and funny.

Unfortunately you cannot take for granted that you know this distinction. I would wager that, until this very moment, you have been assuming that the goal of this book is to persuade you to rely more on your humor nature to provide healing laughter for your self and others around you. That's not exactly true. I really don't care how much you laugh. What I do care about is how much fun you are able to have. If you concentrate on fun, laughter takes care of itself.

So, how do you separate fun from funny? Being funny is a behavior, a performance, if you will. Funny is something said or done with the specific intention of provoking laughter. If laughter is not produced, it is not funny. Consequently, being funny can be hard work indeed. Laughs are not always easy to get, even in the best of circumstances. The set up has to be effective. The timing must be right. You must eliminate irrelevant distractions and, you've got to remember the punch line word for word.

On top of all that, there are certain situations in which it is impossible to be funny, no matter how well you are prepared to “perform.” Under some conditions, laughter may be considered rude, insensitive and even hurtful. The point is, even if you are up to the task, being funny is a skill with limited applications and uncertain results.

On the other hand, having fun is not a “performance.” It is an attitude. Fun is an attitude of willingness to enjoy whatever positive components there are to be found in any circumstance. Willingness is the key, which is very different from willfulness. Fun cannot be forced or fabricated

How might you, for example, execute your attitude of willingness to have fun at a dinner party? You might decide to make a game for yourself out of remembering the names of the other guests. Or, you might want to chuckle inside over the array of soup-eating styles.

What about having fun at the gym? Perhaps you could imagine how the people on the treadmills resemble hamsters that run on those wheels in their cages.

Wherever you may find yourself, the very best way to have fun is to find the common ground with others around you and share your experiences in those areas of commonality. If you are a parent, commiserating with other parents about everything from the “terrible twos” to your teenagers’ messy bedrooms and outlandish music, usually results in a giggle fest over a discovered common bond.

I think you get the picture. You don’t have to be cracking jokes constantly. Fun is often a private experience.

While funny can be unwelcome in some situations, positive energy is never unwelcome. While funny produces laughter, fun is more likely to produce joy, which is a deeper feeling of well being. You can have fun watching a sunset, listening to music, or watching a baby’s smile, even though you may never laugh at those things.

The nervous young woman fidgeted in her chair. It was clear she did not want to be in a psychiatrist's consulting room.

"I'll be honest with you, Dr. Kuhn. The only reason I'm here is because I respect Dr. Adams, my oncologist. I don't have much faith in psychiatry, but she thinks you can help me. She referred to you as the Laugh Doctor. If you're planning to tell me I can laugh away my cancer, I'll just leave right now, and save us both the trouble."

"Why would I tell you to laugh about breast cancer?" I asked quietly. "I don't see anything funny about that. However, I have discovered this to be true: If you can hold onto your sense of humor while you are going through the surgery, the chemotherapy, the fear, uncertainty and pain of it all, you'll do better, live longer and have a better quality of life. If you'll let me, I'd like to help you keep your sense of humor strong and continue to have fun."

"That doesn't make any sense," she countered. "How can I have fun when there's nothing to laugh about?"

"Did you enjoy the sunset last evening?"

"I didn't notice it," she answered.

"That's a shame," I remarked. "It was lovely. I think tonight's will be as well. What about music? Have you heard anything beautiful recently?"

"No, not for a while," she responded. "I think I know where you're going with this."

"Of course you do, and that's my point," I told her. "Fun isn't only about laughter. It's about anything that gives you joy and positive feelings. Sunsets keep happening, whether or not you have cancer. Your favorite music is still going to sound beautiful. Even though you may not feel like laughing, you can still draw positive energy from these things. But, you have to take the time. Don't let cancer dictate every minute. Make sure you see tonight's sunset."

In the weeks and months that followed, I introduced this patient to the strategies you'll learn a bit later in this book—strategies like going the extra smile, turning it over, letting go frequently and finding the pony every day. She learned to use these "techniques" to express her humor nature in some of the most unlikely situations. Once she made balloon animals for everyone in our clinic waiting room, including our receptionist who answered the phone all day wearing a crown made of pink balloons. The giraffe she made for me sat on my desk for a week, until the air went out of its legs.

As she realized that her humor nature was playing a significant role in her recovery, this patient became a staunch advocate of promoting fun. To this day, she makes herself available to help other patients who express doubts about the concept, as she once did.

The key issue is being clear about the difference between fun and funny. It is so easy to blur this distinction. What can happen when we do?

My friend John prides himself on being a funny guy. Recently, he and I ran into a mutual friend, Elizabeth, who looked a bit down.

"How are you?" I inquired.

"A little shell shocked," was her answer. "I just learned yesterday that I have Alzheimer's."

John put his arm around her and said, "My advice is to forget about it."

John laughed, but I noticed Elizabeth didn't.

Then he followed with another "clever" quip. "You know, if you always tell the truth, you don't need a good memory."

More laughter came from John and more silence from Elizabeth.

Elizabeth scowled at John. "Why don't you save your jokes for those who can appreciate them? I'm not ready to laugh yet."

To call this "poor timing" would be an understatement. There are those moments in life for which no joke is helpful, and this was one of them.

John apologized to her. He knew better, but the temptation was just too great to ease his own discomfort over her news with some humor at her expense. A reassuring smile and a hug would have been a much better choice.

Pain is not funny. If someone is in pain, she will not appreciate your attempts to make a joke about it. But, pain need not prevent anyone from having fun. You can still appreciate and even enjoy a warm bath or a gentle massage. And being willing to do so may pay you a bonus dividend by easing the pain somewhat. A sincere hug, a respectful silence, a shared hope, an encouraging word or a gesture of unconditional support can all be effective in promoting the positive energy of well being, without resorting to laughter.

Once you forget funny and concentrate on fun, you will immediately get a taste of your unlimited potential for success and happiness. You will rediscover something you once knew, but have no doubt long forgotten: When it comes to having fun, you never "max out." No matter how much fun you already are (or aren't) having, you can always have a little bit more. You will always be able to turn it up another notch.

I'll illustrate this by describing an exercise that is a popular part of my Laugh Doctor workshops. I call it **"Grin and Share It."** It begins when I ask the participants to raise their hands if they want to have more fun in ten seconds than they are having at the moment. Of course everyone raises a hand (except for those I've already put to sleep).

Then I offer the following suggestions for everyone—feel free to follow these as you read them, that is, if you want to have more fun right now yourself:

"GRIN AND SHARE IT":

Put a smile on your face—and not just any smile. Make it a huge grin from ear to ear. Stretch your face. Look like a cat that just swallowed ten canaries.

Next, while keeping that broad grin on your face, turn and look at the person next to you. (If you are by yourself, keep the grin and look in a mirror.)

While you're grinning and looking at one another (or at your own reflection), point to the person you are looking at and say, "You're funny!"

In my workshops, by the time everyone gets to #3, there is giggling and laughing aplenty. You can feel the upsurge in playfulness and positive energy. Anyone who came to class with a worry on her mind forgets the worry for an instant, if she is willing to participate. Those who are in pain experience a brief moderation in suffering. And everyone feels closer together. For just a second or two, the differences between individuals don't mean as much.

These things never fail to happen when a group becomes willing to have more fun. However, what's most valuable about "Grin and Share It" is that it illustrates three things you will want to remember about fun, so that you can always have as much as you need.

The first is that it proves what we have been saying. Fun is *not* funny. Notice that the "assignment" was not to tell a joke or make your neighbor laugh in some way. Neither did I try to influence laughter from the leadership position. My suggestion was merely to get out of your own way and allow something very natural to occur. As soon as you did that, fun emerged by itself. You did not have to make it happen. You did not have to be funny.

Second, our little "exercise" demonstrates that fun is simply pure positive energy. I think fun is the most powerful positive energy in the world. Some of you may be quick to insist that love deserves that title. I have no argument with that. I think we're really talking about the same thing, because, if it isn't fun, it's not love and, if it isn't love, it's not fun.

The point is, those who state they don't need more fun in their lives are really saying they don't need more positive energy. Have you ever had too much positive energy? I don't think so. When a CEO tells me he doesn't want more fun in his workplace, I suggest that's the kind of thinking that will make his chief competitor more successful.

Finally, "Grin and Share It" reveals the true source of all your potential fun. It shows that the roots of fun do not reside in your surroundings. Your fun comes from within you, inspired and generated by your innate humor nature. The energy you felt during the exercise is energy you carry around inside all the time. We all do. As soon as you became willing, it met you more than halfway.

Thus, if you are saying to yourself, "I'm going to have more fun, once I get that promotion or degree I've been working for," or "I'll have more fun when the kids grow up and leave home," or "I'll have more fun after I lose ten pounds"—cut it out. You are looking in the wrong direction for your fun. It starts inside you.

So now you know that (a) fun isn't funny; (b) fun is pure positive energy; and (c) fun comes from inside you and nowhere else. And all you have to do to remember those three essential characteristics of fun is recall our "Grin and Share It" exercise.

Harrowing events are not funny, but they can be a source of "fun."

In January 2004, Charlotte shattered her L-3 vertebrae into pieces during a freakish sledding accident. Her husband, Brad, vividly remembers getting the phone call that she was in pain and an ambulance was being called. At the time neither had any idea of the extent of her injury. As he drove to meet her in the emergency room, Brad envisioned some time spent in bed on muscle-relaxants, nursing a pulled muscle. A short time later, when the x-rays revealed a broken back, the rug was pulled out from underneath both of them, and their lives were forever altered.

Charlotte endured almost two months in the hospital, unable to get out of bed or even move at all. She had two extremely painful surgeries, and a severe infection between them, before she was finally declared "whole" again. Add to this mix the couple's three children, ages 8, 6, and 5 months, and this was one unsettling, uncertain, and upsetting time.

While there was virtually nothing funny about her process of recovery, Charlotte reports there was actually an incredible amount of fun. Seeing the faces of her children every time Brad brought them to the hospital for a visit wasn't funny, but it sure was fun. Having to depend on her husband in amazingly new and emotionally intimate ways was never funny, but it was very fun. Brad confesses that watching Charlotte take her first unassisted steps, from her hospital bed to her window, was "one of the most fun moments."

When she was able to walk out of the hospital after two months of care, they were both smiling as they recalled that just sixty days earlier neither of them knew if she would ever walk again. Neither told a joke. No one tried to make the other laugh. Nobody exerted an effort to be funny, but seeing their tears of joy and ear-to-ear smiles as she finally walked across their home's threshold would have told you immediately that nothing could ever have equaled the fun of that moment!

Of course you don't have to be going through a life-altering experience to benefit from "finding the positive." If you're stuck in a traffic jam on the highway, it helps to remember that sitting comfortably in your car, even if you're late, sure beats being the one(s) involved in the fender bender.

If it rains on the day of your lawn party, why not have an umbrella sale?

When the washing machine breaks down, donate the clothes to Goodwill. Then buy them back after they are cleaned!

There's fun lurking in any situation.

Just how powerful is this energy we're calling fun?

It's so powerful that I could fill the rest of this book with stories of highly successful people who had no choice but to walk away from their successes when it stopped being fun for them.

Lance Armstrong announced his retirement after winning an unprecedented seventh consecutive Tour de France bicycle race, stating, "It's not fun anymore."

Successful actor, Macaulay Culkin, turned his back on a lucrative motion picture career because "it stopped being fun."

Tiffany Milbrett, a top scorer for the United States Women's National Soccer Team, hung up her cleats at what many regarded as the height of her career, observing, "I'm not having any fun."

Professional golf icon Arnold Palmer said a tearful goodbye to his legions of adoring fans with the observation that he could no longer have fun playing the game.

After a run of only nine years, comedian Jerry Seinfeld decided to pull the plug on his popular television sitcom, *Seinfeld*, while it was still breaking prime time ratings records. "It's time to leave," he said in an interview. "My life is out of balance. I just want to have fun for a few years." Cast member Michael Richards, who played Kramer on the show, put it this way: "It (the show) was becoming work, real work, and we were losing our sense of play."

These are but a few of hundreds of stories, all bearing testimony to the truth that, if you want to succeed at the highest level and you hope to sustain your success over time, you had better make it fun for yourself, and find a way to keep it fun.

Joseph Manckiewicz, the great Hollywood writer, producer and director, once put this truth into a succinct nutshell. When he won multiple Oscars for his film, "All About Eve," in 1951, he was asked the secret of his success as a director. He answered: "Create an atmosphere for fun on the set and you'll always get great work."

I call this *Manckiewicz's Mantra* because I think it has universal applicability. Create an atmosphere for fun and you'll get great communication. Create an atmosphere for fun and you'll get great relationships. Create an atmosphere for fun and you'll get great health. In this sense, all business, including the business of life itself, is indeed show business and this powerful truth applies without exception across the board.

You can be sure that the lesson has not been lost on my friend, Jerry Lewis. He and Dean Martin had the most successful comedy team in show business history. They broke up in 1956 because, Jerry Lewis says today, they "stopped having fun."

My patient Maureen was waging a losing battle with gastrointestinal cancer. Her son, Henry, was serving with the Marines in Iraq and was not due to come home for eight months. The problem was that Maureen's doctors were telling her she had only a few more weeks to live. Nevertheless, she was determined to keep going until Henry got home safely. She was convinced that his knowing that she would be waiting for him would inspire him to do whatever was necessary to survive his ordeals of battle.

She managed to stay alive those many months, although, as you might imagine, it was very tough. To the amazement of her doctors, and with the help of strong pain medication, she clung to life dramatically. Even on her worst days she was able to share her positive spirit and her hope with those at her bedside. On the day of Henry's return, she was practically comatose. Her life seemed to be hanging by the proverbial "thread."

But, when her son walked into her bedroom, she literally came alive. They hugged. They cried. They laughed together. Although it had been more than a week since she had been able to keep food on her stomach, Maureen ate a meal with her son.

That night she did not need her pain medication. She fell asleep peacefully for the first time in months, and in the midst of that restful slumber, took her last breath.

Folks, I can't think of a more convincing illustration of the extraordinary power of fun. Maureen had a positive reason to live beyond all rational expectations: the joy of seeing her son come home from the battlefield alive. Given that opportunity, her humor nature rose to the challenge and never looked back. Please understand that we are all capable of such miracles.

Have you ever stopped to consider just how many choices you have at any time for expressing your humor nature? If you're like most people, you are in the habit of assuming that laughter is your only option. Yet, you now know that at times fun doesn't even involve laughter. So, what are your options?

Stretching from the subtlest to the most intense, I have identified no less than 16 different expressions that can be used to communicate humor and fun. All of them deserve to be included in your personal arsenal.

1. There is the **smirk**, which is the subtlest expression of humor known to mankind. It involves a very slight broadening of your mouth

and the gentlest hint of openness in your eyes. Only those who are intensely looking for it will ever notice a smirk on your face.

2. Next is a **smile**, silent, but as we have noted, quite profound. A smile is non-intrusive, but nonetheless easily noticed. The corners of your mouth are up-turned and there is a sparkle in your eyes.

3. One step up from a smile, we find the **grin**. Grinning is really a smile into which additional facial muscles have been recruited. The corners of your mouth are stretched upward and outward. Your cheeks are involved, and your eyes are narrowed and "soft". With the broadest grin, your ears actually tilt back.

4. The next step is a **snicker**, which is your first audible level of humor expression. A snicker is sort of a grin accompanied by staccato bursts of air released from your nose. It's sometimes useful for clearing out your sinuses.

5. A **titter** is nothing more than a snicker that has found its voice. As such it is slightly louder and higher pitched than its predecessor. At this point you are approaching the upper limits of voluntary control. A strong titter can be difficult to suppress.

6. A breakthrough is achieved with the next gradation—the **giggle**. This delightful expression combines all of the previous steps and adds a deeper louder voice, involving your neck and chest ever so slightly. When you reach this level of involvement, your humor nature is capable of taking over completely. We have all experienced the frustration of attempting to suppress a giggle. The harder you try, the stronger the giggle becomes, often to your utter embarrassment.

7. Moving up the ladder from a giggle, you will encounter the **chuckle**, which resembles the sound of a dog whose bark is caught in his throat. The chuckle is distinctly louder than its predecessor, but its sound may not be detectable beyond the confines of a relatively small grouping of people. The sound of your chuckle comes primarily from the back of your throat.

8. The **chortle** is an escalation of a chuckle in both volume and depth. Think of Ed McMahon's responses during Johnny Carson's monologues on the Tonight Show. That's a chortle, a sound that originates from deep in your chest and is loud enough to fill a room. Santa Claus is another famous example of the chortle in action.

9. At last you reach the level of a **laugh**. You may have previously used this term more generically to describe almost any expression of your *humor nature*, but now that you have a connoisseur's appreciation of the menu, you can be more precise. A laugh is an energetic and rhythmic expression of amusement that involves your head, neck and torso.

By the time you have reached the level of laughter, you are no longer in control. Laughter is not only unrestrained, but also infectious. You cannot help but go along with it. The sound of laughter comes from deep in your chest, but unlike the chortle, it has an unrestricted range and volume. A laugh has a definite rhythm and is often quite melodic. It has been said that laughter is God's music. But there's more—much more.

10. Turning the dial another notch higher, you will encounter the **cackle**. A cackle is a laugh on pep pills—more energetic and higher pitched than its predecessor. If your torso isn't already shaking with laughter, it surely gets a workout with a cackle.

11. The next gradation in humor expression is a **guffaw**. When things reach this level of intensity, your entire body is involved—arms, legs, and sometimes certain sphincters. A guffaw is loud and strong. It is incompatible with a full bladder.

The guffaw is probably the strongest humor expression you can make by yourself. However, if you are in the presence of other people, there are even more intense experiences to be had.

12, 13. A **howl** and a **shriek** are the next escalations. Both communicate a sense of being overwhelmed by fun nearly to the point of saturation. When you have reached the level of howling and shrieking with others, it's as if you're saying, "Enough! Let me catch my breath. I can't laugh any harder."

But you can.

14. A **roar** is a group phenomenon. Individuals may howl and shriek when they are intensely amused, but only a crowd can roar. When you are swept up with roaring laughter, individual differences are momentarily lost and you are of one mind and voice with everyone involved.

15. Yet there is still a higher point to be reached. To **convulse** in laughter is the most all-encompassing expression of amusement. Every part of your physical being is overcome by laughter. You have lost control completely. If you are standing, you must sit down. If you are already sitting, you are likely to end up on the floor. If it hasn't happened already, now is when normal continence is lost.

16. Which brings us to the epitome of laughter intensity, the act of **"dying"**—"I *died* laughing" is the way we describe this incomparable experience. The term is of course used figuratively, but the allusion is apt. Once you have experienced this level of laughter, you are

physically and emotionally spent. You have nothing left. In the moments that immediately follow, you experience a rebirth of sorts. Like a newborn infant, you may be physically weak and lack coordination. At the same time, all of your senses may be refreshed and sharpened. And, in some instances, you may need a change of underwear.

A member of my *humor nature* network sent me this account of an intense fun reaction within her family that involved several of the sixteen "stages of laughter" I just described:

This week my husband and daughter were standing in the kitchen while I was making a cake. Out of the blue, my husband said to my daughter, "Did you know that if you sneeze, fart and cough at the same time, you will die?"

I said, "You will what?"

"You will die," he repeated.

At that moment I began to laugh so hard I was squealing. Tears were running down my face. I couldn't stop, and when I would try to stop it would start up again. I began to stagger around the kitchen like a drunken person, still holding the batter spoon. Everyone was laughing so hard and, oh, it felt so good.

Actually what triggered the whole thing was remembering a girl in high school who had done two of the three, and I was visualizing the scene all over again. I couldn't imagine her doing all three. She probably would have just fallen out of her chair.

Here's a scene I witnessed involving two of my childhood friends.

Brothers Frank and Jeffrey were testing their father's patience with their bickering. Finally, they reached his limit and he said, "Boys, this is your last warning. If I hear one more word, I'm taking off my belt, and you know what's going to happen then."

Jeffrey replied, "Yeah, your pants will fall down."

Their father was laughing so hard he could not have mustered the strength or the resolve to give them a whipping that day.

There you have it—reasons aplenty to elevate your humor attitude to the level you need for unleashing your humor nature for extraordinary health and success. By now, I'm guessing that you're chomping at the bit to get moving on this whole process. So, I invite you to turn the page and begin Step 4, which initiates the second phase of the HA HA HA Prescription—Reviving Your Humor Aptitude.

Step Four: Unleash Your Humor Nature

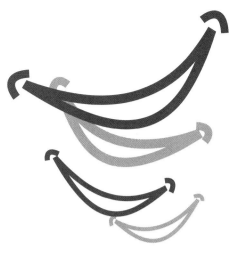

"At the height of laughter, the universe is flung into a kaleidoscope of new possibilities." —*Jean Houston*

If you are willing to trust your humor nature to deliver the goods every time, you will quickly rediscover that you have never lost your capacity for having fun—your **humor aptitude**. It is poised to carry you to great heights, once you give it the green light. This is wonderful news to the part of you that wants to be excellent.

What do we mean by humor aptitude? An aptitude is a natural inclination, a "hard-wired" competency that can only be expanded, never diminished. Some people have a natural aptitude for playing music. Others might have a special aptitude for physical sports. Maybe you have an aptitude for writing poetry, crunching numbers, or drawing pictures. You may cultivate your aptitudes or you may choose to let them lie dormant, but you can never lose them. In addition to the natural gifts you have already identified in your repertoire, there is one aptitude that you share with every reader of this book, without exception. It is your natural inclination for humor and fun—your humor aptitude.

As surely as fish have a natural aptitude for swimming, birds for flying, and politicians for passing the buck, so too is every human being endowed from birth with a natural gift for creating fun. You are perfectly suited for creating an "atmosphere for fun" everywhere you go. You can be a "Pied Piper" of fun.

Joseph loves to dance. Whenever there is a social function that includes dancing as part of the evening, he and his wife are the first to arrive and the last to leave.

The instant the band sounds its first note, he is on the dance floor and he dances non-stop throughout the night—slow dancing, fast dancing and everything in between. Joseph seemingly cannot get enough of what for him is a sublime activity. He appears totally unselfconscious, surrendering his body and spirit completely to the rhythms and tones of the music. His eyes close, as he is transported by the beat, and he seems to become more energetic and animated the longer he stays on the floor. It is fun just to watch him.

There is one tiny flaw in this picture of Joseph I am painting for you. He has no apparent aptitude for dancing. That's right. He seems to have been born with the proverbial "two left feet." He is awkward and at times out of control. Quite often it appears impossible for his partner to follow his lead. Women come back from a turn on the floor with Joseph with his footprints all over their shoes.

However, none of these things seem to matter, because it is a joy to be in his presence when he is dancing. Although he has no aptitude whatsoever for dancing, Joseph has a strongly developed aptitude for fun that transcends his two left feet. Everyone in the room is glad he is on the dance floor. He invigorates us all with his enthusiastic exuberance.

The lesson here is that Joseph gives in so completely to his ecstatic joy on the dance floor that his "technical" shortcomings become irrelevant. That is exactly what will happen for you and me whenever we are willing and able to surrender to our unleashed humor natures. Therefore, the key to rediscovering and strengthening your humor aptitude is in learning to surrender to it, which, though simple, is not easy.

To surrender, however, there are barriers we must overcome:

THE DESIRE FOR CONTROL

How does a control freak surrender? He kicks and screams and fights for as long as possible. Control freaks don't so much surrender as have things torn from their grasp.

So, if you are obsessed with control, I suggest you pick your fights wisely. You know you can't win every time. And for goodness sake, once you realize you're beaten, have the common sense to throw in the towel and save your strength for the next battle, because, in that instance, surrendering gracefully is the closest you're going to get to being in control.

THE DESIRE TO BE STRONG

Maybe you're one of those people who think of surrender as a sign of weakness. Surrender is not about strength versus weakness; it is about power versus powerlessness. When a policeman pulls you over for speeding, you might be bigger and stronger than he, but you would be wise to surrender, because he has all the power at that moment. Exercising your superior strength would only get you in deeper trouble. Banging your head repeatedly against a stone wall is not an exercise of strength. It is ignorance of the reality that you are powerless to knock the wall down. Whenever you surrender, you are acknowledging that you are powerless, and it takes a strong person to do that. It is the weak person who cannot surrender, because he needs the power to make up for his lack of strength.

SHEER STUBBORNNESS

Some of us are emotional bullies. We insist on having our way, no matter what. We're so infatuated by our own ideas, we can't imagine any other way. If you fit this category, you're going to find out, if you haven't already, that "my way or the highway" is a poor strategy for success and happiness. The sooner you share some of the load, the happier and healthier you're going to be.

ATTACHMENT TO FAMILIARITY

We are creatures of habit. We want things to be familiar and predictable. While this might be understandable, however, it is also unhealthy. You will never be at your best if you always do everything the same way. Remember what a wise man once said: "The only difference between a rut and a grave is the depth." If you're stuck in a hole, the first thing to do is stop your digging. That is a form of surrender.

FEAR OF UNCERTAINTY

Surrender usually means that something or someone other than you is going to be in charge. This makes it difficult to anticipate what's coming next. You can't see the trail that lies ahead. The future is uncertain and you feel insecure.

If that is your concern, realize this: The future has always been and will always be uncertain. When you surrender, you are simply placing the energy you have used to try to control it into making quicker adaptations to the unforeseen events that will occur.

Now, let's talk about surrender itself. Surrender is an act of giving *in*, not of giving *up*. Once again we have run into two concepts that are easy to confuse. Surrendering does not mean giving up all your options. It simply means recognizing the reality that some things are beyond your control. **Surrendering is an act of preserving your viable options,** not abandoning them.

Grady, a physician specializing in internal medicine, was diagnosed with insulin-dependent diabetes at age 45. Eighteen months later he described his progress in adjusting to the demands of his disease:

"For the first several months I was furious at God and myself, and jealous of everybody else," he recalled. "It didn't seem fair. I had worked really hard to develop my practice and to reach the status I was enjoying amongst my colleagues. Nobody handed it to me. I had earned the right to my lifestyle, and now it was being taken away. I remember thinking there was no use in persisting, if that was all it would come to. Then, I began to listen to my patients, many of whom had more severe restrictions than I, and I felt ashamed of myself for all my whining.

"So, I decided I had to make a choice. Either I could go on being resentful, angry, resistant and reluctant about my fate, or I could give in to the positive perspective, which is that I had a game plan for managing my illness and a way to monitor my day-to-day success in following it. I could be grateful for what I still had, rather than obsessing about what I'd lost. As soon as I surrendered to the more positive perspective, I noticed I immediately had more energy and enthusiasm for everything, and my family seemed to find me easier to be around."

"Don't get me wrong," he added. "I still would rather not have diabetes. It's just a little easier to take since I switched my attitude."

As soon as Grady surrendered to a "more positive perspective," he noticed more energy and enthusiasm for everything. You can experience this same surge of energy from surrendering, and it needn't involve something as serious as a life-altering illness.

Suppose your mother-in-law is coming for a visit. If she's a difficult person to get along with, where's the positive in that? Well, maybe it's in thinking about how much your father-in-law might be enjoying the chance to be alone for a few days. Or there's the thought that "it could be worse." What if she lived with you permanently? Now you're viewing her visit in a more positive perspective.

Maybe you're dreading a dental appointment. Where's the positive? Think of how clean your teeth will be when you leave. Think of how clever you are in taking steps to avoid painful dental problems down the road. Think of how in just an hour or so you will *have already gone* to the dentist, which is a much more satisfying feeling. Like pregnancy, **surrender is an all or nothing situation.** Giving in to your humor nature takes a commitment from your entire being—nothing held back. No half measures will be successful. Haven't you noticed that genuine success in anything always takes an all-out effort?

John Wooden is a fiercely competitive man. In case you are one of the very few people who do not recognize his name, he was the head coach of men's basketball at UCLA from 1948 to 1974. During that time, this remarkable gentleman coached his teams to no less than 10 NCAA Division I championships and at one point compiled a string of 88 consecutive victories, a record which may never be equaled. Called the Wizard of Westwood, John Wooden is regarded by many as the best college coach ever.

Coach Wooden writes in his autobiography that, despite his competitive nature, he always derived more satisfaction from coaching a team that lost while playing up to its full potential, than from a team that won while giving only a partial effort. To him the quality and intensity of effort was always more valuable than the results on the scoreboard. He defines true success as the satisfaction of performing at maximum effort, to the limits of one's skill, regardless of the outcome. In his view, when maximum effort is given, there are no losers.

Surrender is a bona fide success strategy. It only looks like a step backward when you can't see the whole picture. Surrendering is really an exercise that realigns you with forces and energy that can take you further and lift you higher than you could ever imagine. Remember how Charlie Chaplin put it: "Life is tragedy in close up; but, comedy in long shot."

Two bulls were standing together on a hillside overlooking a meadow in which six cows were grazing.

The youngest turned to his mate and said: "Those cows look mighty sexy from here. Let's charge on down there and have our way with a couple of them."

The older and wiser bull thought for a moment and then replied:

"I've got a better idea. Let's walk down and have our way with all of them."

When Max arrived at the airport gate for his flight, he encountered a friend who was taking the same flight to attend the same meeting as he. As they sat catching up on old times, it was announced that their departure would be delayed for two hours due to mechanical difficulties.

"Come on," said his friend, charging up to the ticket counter.

"My friend and I have to be in Orlando tonight," she told the agent, "What other arrangements can you make for us?" The agent was most reassuring. "Don't worry. This flight will get you there tonight. It will just be two hours later than scheduled."

"Not good enough," quipped Max's friend. "We need another flight now."

The agent re-routed them on a flight through Dallas that got them in later than their scheduled flight would have, even with the two-hour delay.

Max had to admit he thought they were going to a lot of trouble for nothing.

"I've seen this too many times," his friend reassured him, "There's only a fifty-fifty chance that the mechanical problems will get fixed in time. If not, they'll cancel the flight, and by that time, there will be no way to get there tonight. We're better off taking the higher odds, even though it's going to take longer."

Of course, Max couldn't resist calling the airline the next day to find out what happened to his original flight. It had been cancelled after a second two-hour delay, because the crew was unavailable once the plane was fixed. Without his friend's quick footwork—and his willingness to surrender to her greater expertise—Max might have still been sitting in the airport waiting.

Max was glad he went along with his friend's aggressive plan, but he admits he would never have done it without her. As he thought about his reluctance at the time, part of it had to do with his relative inexperience as an airline traveler. But that wasn't all of it. He remembers not wanting to give up the convenience of the original, more familiar, flight. Not only was it to have been a direct flight to Orlando, but, even with the proposed delay, it was expected to get him there sooner than the alternative.

In short, Max had become *mired in an attachment to his original plan*. Had it not been for his friend's ability to promptly surrender on his behalf to the alternative arrangement, he would have been stranded that night. It makes me wonder how many times in life

I may have unknowingly "stranded" myself by failing to promptly give in to reality and surrender my cherished expectations.

How about you? Has it ever happened that you were reluctant to give up your cherished way of doing something only to discover a new way worked just as well, or even better? Do you look back on that sweetheart who stood you up years ago and thank him for preventing you from settling for less than the relationship you have now? How many times and in how many ways would you have settled for less, if not pushed by circumstances to reach for more?

Climbing out of the mire of your limited expectations is the challenge that we are addressing in this chapter. It requires nothing less than your unconditional surrender to your humor nature. It requires real commitment.

Four senior medical students signed up for my month-long course in humor and healing.

Sarah was there because her academic advisor had told her she needed to "lighten up." She attended every class session, completed every assignment and became conversant in the terminology of humor. When the course ended, I never heard from Sarah again.

Susan was interested in applying for a residency position in our department and thought it would be helpful to spend some academic time with the residency training director (me). She carried out every assignment in a timely fashion and even volunteered to help me make copies of various documents for inclusion in the syllabus. When the course ended, Susan applied for our residency, got in, and despite frequent opportunities to discuss progress over the years, never mentioned humor to me again.

Sam expressed a deep interest in and fascination with the process of humor and its beneficial effects. At the end of my course, he wrote a paper on the topic of humor, which he asked me to review and edit. Together we produced a manuscript that he was able to get published. Sam is now a successful practicing physician and I hear from him occasionally.

Stephanie was diagnosed with cancer six months before my tutorial. She signed up to learn how humor could play a greater role in her recovery. She absorbed the information like a sponge, asking questions about the variety of ways to implement the smile strategies we studied. She considered her sense of humor to be essential in her cancer recovery and to this day continues to apply humor liberally in both her practice and her personal life. She visits me regularly to "check in," sharing her experiences with humor and seeking my guidance. To Stephanie, humor has literally become a matter of life or death.

It's not enough to merely comply with your humor nature. I've watched many people go along with the "fun commandments" I am about to teach you, either because they sounded like fun or because they had some trust in my expertise when I endorsed them. Typically, these people experience some momentary relief, but it doesn't last very long. Just going along won't bring you the success you seek, because **compliance is not commitment.** My student Sarah was an example of compliance.

I've even seen participants in my workshops go a step further and become willing to cooperate with their humor natures. They will actually do their assignments with enthusiasm and dedication. They are not just going along with the flow. They are putting some of their own energy into the mix. Like my student Susan, who exemplified cooperation, they get a little more out of their efforts. *Cooperation* is better than compliance, but when it comes to unleashing your humor aptitude, it still *doesn't qualify as commitment.*

Maybe, like Sam, my student collaborator, you have passed those two stages and reached a level of true collaboration with your humor nature. You have become more than cooperative. You have embraced the spirit of humor as your own and become a co-creator, at times even an initiator, of the fun that swirls around you. However, you continue to reserve for yourself the ultimate veto power anytime you don't like the direction in which your humor aptitude takes you. Even though you are humor's collaborator, you remain in charge of when and where you"use"your humor nature. Alas, *collaboration* may be a sign of great progress for you, but *it is still not commitment.*

Compliance, cooperation and collaboration will serve to bring you to the brink of the commitment you will need, but it requires surrender to get you over the hurdle. With good reason, my student Stephanie was able to surrender and commit herself to humor. Surrender means subjecting yourself to the dictates of your humor nature. It means serving humor, not using it. It means trusting that your natural aptitude will take you where you need to be, even if that is different from where you want to end up. It means, as with Stephanie, making fun your top priority at all times.

Why is this level of absolute surrender necessary? It is because we are now talking about something you can't *make* happen, no matter how hard you try. You can only step aside and *allow* it to happen naturally. "We will have fun, and that's an order," is no way to create the healthy, energetic atmosphere you seek. You have to get out of your own way.

It will be easier to give in to your humor nature if you can remember the difference between having fun (an attitude) and being funny (a performance). Recall that funny is a narrow concept that is not always helpful to you or those around you. In contrast, fun is a much broader and deeper energy that is more reliable and trustworthy. Fun is really another name for joy, optimism and indeed wellness.

Having fun is the antecedent to all success—physical, mental, spiritual and social. Therefore, the objective of your surrender is to have fun first in everything. It is easy to confuse this commitment with Garfield's advice, "Life is short, so eat dessert first!" However, that would be a misinterpretation. This strategy advocates making everything you do "sweet" enough that it could be a dessert. That way, every "course" is a dessert course. You don't have to postpone your enjoyment until the end of the meal.

For example, let's say you have three activities on your agenda this morning: (a) vacuuming the house; (b) washing a load of clothes; and (c) going for a walk. And let's assume you're not looking forward to the first two at all; whereas you are wildly enthusiastic about the walk. You may think you have only two choices for completion of this agenda: (1) grit your teeth and trudge through the vacuuming and the wash, holding the walk in your mind as a reward for your sacrifice, or (2) take the walk first, hoping the energy it gives you will help you get through the other two tasks (or hoping that the house will burn down while you're walking, relieving you of the vacuuming and washing, at least for that day).

Having fun first is actually a third alternative. It means doing whatever you can to make the vacuuming and the washing fun, so that you don't have to put off fun until your walk. You might try vacuuming to music and see if you can keep up with the rhythm of the tune or try to finish a section of the house before the tune ends. Perhaps you can make a game out of sorting the wash. Do the matched socks outnumber the unmatched ones? Who gets the prize for the most T-shirts worn this week?

Anything that helps you pass the drudgery time more pleasantly will add energy to your day, even before you get to take your walk. Be resolved to find fun in every moment. Only then will you be consistently at your best.

This of course sounds like a selfish strategy, and guess what—it is. You really have no choice. You have to be selfish if you want to enjoy your best health and optimum success. No one is going to do it for you. Don't confuse this with being self-centered. Selfish and self-centered are not the same thing.

Selfish means keeping your own needs uppermost at all times in your priorities—thinking of yourself first. Self-centered means insisting that the whole world revolve around you—that *everybody* must think of you first. You are not everybody's responsibility. You are your own. And, there's nothing wrong with the question, "What's in it for me?"

If the answer is "not much fun," it's probably time to move on.

You will remember we pointed out that fun originates from within each of us. That means that the roots of pure fun lie in your heart, not in your mind. You cannot think your way to happiness. All your ideas about it are counterfeit. To experience true joy and happiness, you must **get out of your mind and into your heart.**

Like the song from Damn Yankees says, "Oh, it's fine to be a genius, of course, but put that old horse before the cart. First, ya gotta have heart!" All fun begins in the heart. So, it follows that your natural humor aptitude comes from your heart as well. Your mind is much too control-oriented to produce such nonsense. The unleashing of your humor nature really comes down to the unleashing of your heart, and that's where total surrender becomes essential.

You see, your heart only knows two speeds: standing still or going a bazillion miles an hour—nothing in between. Either it is not involved at all or it takes over completely. *(Talk about uncompromising!)* Even though we use the term frequently, there is no such thing as a half-hearted effort. "Half-hearted" usually means compliance (just going along), which doesn't involve your heart at all and won't get you much lasting success.

Half measures, compromise, speed limits—these are all products of your mind and they have almost nothing to do with fun. In this sense, your heart is usually at odds with your mind. Your mind will at times give "token" recognition to your heart's point of view, but there is a basic conflict of focus between the two. Whereas your mind is preoccupied with what you want, your heart is focused on what you actually need. The conflict goes even deeper. Your mind constantly asks the question, "What am I to *do*?" In contrast, your heart asks, "What am I to *be*?"

Here's another difference between your heart and your mind. Mind speaks up and is even capable of shouting. Heart never speaks louder than a whisper. That means when heart and mind are in active conflict, all you are likely to hear is the shouting of your mind. To hear your heart, you usually have to be very quiet.

In unleashing your humor aptitude, you are indeed following your heart. Since it knows what you need, it will always lead you to where you need to be, the place or situation in which you will be the happiest, healthiest and most successful.

Now it may not be the place you had in mind. That is why complete commitment to your humor aptitude is essential. You may be called upon to surrender your cherished agenda and embrace something new.

As a sophomore at college, David was a high jumper and hurdler on the track team. His roommates were on the soccer team. They urged him to try out for the soccer team, because they knew he could jump and they needed a goalie. He resisted because he knew nothing about the game and was afraid he would embarrass them and himself as well. They persisted. Finally, he heard his heart tell him that even if he wasn't very good, it would be fun to have more in common with his two best friends. Soccer turned out to be even more fun than David could have imagined, and by his senior year he was successful enough to be selected as an Honorable Mention All-American at his position.

Was he ever glad he listened to his heart!

To be fully committed, you must make a conscious choice to follow your heart instead of your mind. You must start each thought and behavior from your heart. It is easier to do this if you are already residing in your heart.

So, I challenge you to get out of your mind and into your heart. The best way to do this is to **spend some time each day in absolute silence.** Perhaps that's not your style, but I assure you that it pays valuable dividends physically, mentally and spiritually.

All you have to do is sit still in a quiet place and listen only to your own breathing, in and out. Resist the urge to think of things. Your mind will want to take advantage of the down time to go over some things you've been thinking about or planning to do. Just keep turning that off as you turn off your TV or radio. Keep your attention on your breath, and sit that way for a few minutes, listening to nothing. When you finish, you won't feel dramatically different, and I doubt if you will have actually heard an "inner voice." However, without realizing it, you will walk away with a little more trust in your intuition. Each time you do this, your trust in the "unspoken" guidance of your heart will grow a little more. It won't be too long before you notice that this guidance is playing a larger role in the choices you make. Gradually, you will be listening less to your mind and more to your heart—spending more time out of your mind.

Do not confuse this with losing your mind. That is quite a different thing and not to be recommended. Your mind, with its abundance of information and technical brilliance, is a major contributor to your success. You don't want to lose that, but you do want to subject it to the dictates of your heart. In other words, you want and need your mind along for the ride, but you don't need it to be in the driver's seat. That position can be awarded to your heart.

This will require a new way of thinking and speaking about

your behavior style. Instead of diving in "head first," you'll go "heart first."You'll give up being "headstrong" in favor of becoming "heartstrong."When making preparations for anything, you'll seek a "hearts up"instead of the habitual"heads up."Remembering that your heart "speaks" only in whispers, starting with heart means taking a moment to be quiet before embarking on any enterprise, so you can listen to what your heart has to "say."

Your mind is a reference book; your heart is a map. When you are in the heat of action, you need a map, not an encyclopedia. So, stop trying to use your mind like a map. No wonder you're not having any fun.

Your forgotten humor aptitude is residing in your heart right this minute. To identify and reconnect with it, you will need"heartfirst" strategies. All of the smile strategies you will learn in Step Five, beginning with "going the extra smile," are heartfirst strategies. And, as you practice such strategies, you will discover that when you are in your heart, you are indeed out of your mind. They can't both be in charge. Others will notice the difference and may ask you, "Are you out of your mind?" Now that you know that is a good thing, you will be able to answer, "Yes I am, and thank you for noticing!"

Starting with your heart produces many benefits. For one, it makes you a safer person for others to be with. Do you get the sense that others are comfortable around you now? Do you think they feel safe interacting with you? Or do you sense that people are guarded and defensive when talking with you?

Linda had a great deal of difficulty understanding why her friends never seemed very appreciative of the things she would do for them. It had reached the point that she was feeling abused and resented it.

She saw herself as generous with her time and resources whenever a friend needed her. What she could not see was that, even though she had the best of intentions, she had a habit of taking over the situation whenever a friend brought a problem to her. Instead of listening and offering support, she was inclined to make snap judgments and dictate the solutions she thought best, at times taking matters into her own hands, even over her friends' objections.

I asked her a simple question. "Linda, what is it that you need from these friends?"

She thought for a moment before answering, "I need them to respect and appreciate what I offer them."

"What if they need the same thing?"

My second question confused Linda, until I explained that when her friends came to her with their problems, they might be looking for something other than quick solutions. Perhaps they shared her need to be respected and appreciated. I pointed out that sometimes taking over another person's problem, even with the best of intentions, sends a message of disrespect. If people do not feel respected they may have difficulty being grateful for the advice. I asked Linda to think about how her propensity to take over her friends' problems could be making them feel unsafe around her.

Heart to heart is the best way to achieve a mutually non-threatening (as in fearless) connection with other people. Minds compete, whereas hearts connect. Minds are into one-upsmanship; hearts are into oneness. Starting with your heart and "speaking" from your heart are the best ways to encourage others to do the same. This creates a safe interpersonal environment that inevitably leads to a more successful outcome.

Collaborative effort never occurs in the presence of fear. The more openhearted you are, the less fearful others will be. In this sense your humor aptitude "levels the playing field" for all concerned.

I was lying on my doctor's examining table waiting for my annual physical examination, or, as I like to call it, the updated estimate of damages. Bursting into the room, as if shot from a cannon, came the EKG technician. It didn't appear as though her day was going as smoothly as she had planned it. She seemed to be under some time pressure.

Without making eye contact, she muttered a quick, "Good morning," and went immediately to the cardiogram machine.

Standing with her back to me, she started asking for information to write on the EKG tracing.

"Name?"

I told her.

"Age?"

Again, I answered.

"Sex?" she inquired, in a voice that indicated she knew that was a silly question.

I paused, and then responded. "Well, OK. But could you turn down the lights and put on some music?"

As we both laughed, there was eye contact for the first time, and the "playing field" became even.

You may be thinking that anecdote doesn't have anything to do with open heartedness. It's just an example of how a good joke relieves tension and removes anonymity. I think it's more than that, and here's why.

When the interaction began, the technician and I were two people who were disconnected. She was treating me like a "statistic" and I was treating her like a machine ("just the facts, ma'am"). The humor in the joke opened both of our hearts and allowed us to connect on a new and more mutual level.

There is nothing better than humor for creating, often without words, a heart to heart connection between people. A genuine smile will open your heart every time.

Practicing the discipline of giving full attention to your heart will benefit you in another way. Besides serving to unleash the incredible energy and creativity of your natural humor aptitude, it will also keep you firmly grounded in the present moment. You see, it is your mind that likes to linger over the past and project into the future. Your heart cares only about the here and now. When you quiet the chatter of your mind, all you have left to consider is the present moment. You will not waste precious energy worrying about what should have happened in the past or what ought to happen next. You will be in a position to deal with life on life's terms, an approach shared by every truly successful person.

In his best-selling book, *Good To Great*, author Jim Collins describes something he calls the "Stockdale Paradox," which he identifies as a common characteristic of great enterprise.

The Stockdale Paradox is drawn from the experience of Admiral James Stockdale, who was the highest-ranking United States military officer in the "Hanoi Hilton" prisoner-of-war camp during the height of the Vietnam War. Stockdale survived an eight-year imprisonment from 1965 to 1973, which included many instances of torture and, of course, no certainty of ever seeing his loved ones again.

In an interview with Collins, the Admiral described what saw him through that horrendous experience: "I never lost faith in the end of the story ... that I would prevail in the end."

Stockdale went on to describe the ones who didn't get through it as "optimists," by which he meant people who pinned all their hopes on being released by a certain deadline. The deadlines came and went and they "died of a broken heart."

Stockdale summarized the "paradox" as follows:

"You must never confuse faith that you will prevail in the end—which you can never afford to lose—with the discipline to confront the most brutal facts of your current reality, whatever they might be."

Collins went on to make the following observation:

> "The Stockdale Paradox is a signature of all those who create greatness, be it in leading their own lives or in leading others. Churchill had it during the Second World War. Admiral Stockdale, like Viktor Frankl before him, lived in a prison camp. And while our good-to-great companies cannot claim to have experienced either the grandeur of saving the free world or the depth of personal experience of living in a POW camp, they all embraced the Stockdale Paradox. It didn't matter how bleak the situation or how stultifying their mediocrity, they all maintained unwavering faith that they would not just survive, but prevail as a great company. And yet, at the same time, they became relentlessly disciplined at confronting the most brutal facts of their current reality.
>
> If you are able to adopt this dual pattern, you will dramatically increase the odds of making a series of good decisions and ultimately discovering a simple, yet deeply insightful, concept for making the really big choices."

(Collins, J.C., Good To Great, HarperCollins, NY, NY, 2001)

Your heart is always clear about what you need. So, by starting with heart, you will be in closer touch with your needs than your wants, which is the surest preparation for success you will ever find. You may at times think your heart is leading you "the long way around," but you can rest assured it knows the most effective and efficient path.

My brother Douglas loved sailing and was quite an accomplished helmsman. As I recall the times I spent with him on his sailboat, it gives me a fresh understanding of the "art" of surrendering. Before "shoving off," he would always offer his passengers a minor philosophical "treatise" on the tactic of tacking.

"Now, we have two choices for how we're going to get from here to our destination," he would say as he launched the boat. "We can take the sail down and row a straight line to it. If we choose that, it will take forever and we'll be totally exhausted when we get there. Or, we can put up the sail and zigzag our way, tacking back and forth against the wind. Even though that's not as direct, we'll get there sooner and we'll have energy left for other things."

"But what if the wind is blowing against us?" was the usual question.

"Watch and learn", he would reply.

Of course, the correct choice was obvious. It was a sailboat, not a rowboat. The payoff, as he would always point out, was that, by giving in to the less direct route, even though at times it pointed the boat away from the destination, the passengers were able to enjoy the exhilarating energy of the wind propelling them faster and further than they could have gone on their own—and it was more fun.

Like Joseph on the dance floor and Douglas in his boat, now is your time to give in to your healthy humor aptitude and make fun your highest priority.

Step Five: Practice the Smile Strategies

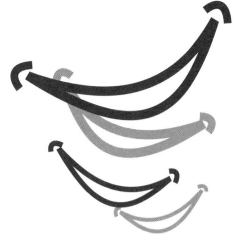

Your natural aptitude for humor springs forth effortlessly when you practice heart-first strategies every day. In this chapter I will enumerate 52 smile strategies. This is designed to give you a new one to work on each week for an entire year.

Every strategy focuses on a different aspect of your natural aptitude for creating fun. Each will introduce you to a mindset that will encourage your humor nature to be active and strong, allowing you to unleash the full power of your positive energy.

The good news is that none of the strategies require you to do anything you haven't done before. You won't have to acquire any new skills—just brush up on some that you may not have used recently. A smile strategy is an opportunity to frame each of life's moments in your mind in a way that gains maximum benefits from your natural medicine: humor.

If you practice the smile strategies enough, you'll soon find that they become a part of your life. That's the beauty of this approach. Each one is like a new judo move in your arsenal of humor "martial arts." However, instead of defeating evil ninja assassins, you're defeating a much more dangerous and threatening enemy—your seriousness.

The advantage of developing a repertoire of 52 strategies is, whenever you find one not working, you'll have two or three others to turn to that will. Never again will you be cut off from your *humor nature.*

So, without further fanfare, here are the smile strategies. Practice each one for a week, and by the end of one year, you will have quite a repertoire to draw from. There is no particular order of preference, except that the first one on the list is obviously the most basic strategy of them all.

• ALWAYS GO THE EXTRA SMILE •

The cornerstone of your aptitude for humor and fun is your smile. "A smile," musician/comedian Victor Borge said, "is the shortest distance between two people." It is the "ground floor" of all your social skills, the vehicle through which you first reached out to others around you. Smiling connects your heart directly to the hearts of others without a word being uttered.

As powerful as it is, this may be the easiest strategy to overlook. Admit it. You do not smile as often or for as long as you could. Why? Because you've "outsourced" the initiation of your smile. "Sure, I'll smile—as soon as there is something to smile about."

In case you haven't noticed, you can go days at a stretch without something happening to provoke your smile. However, trusting "outside" stimuli to get you smiling offers about the same odds as hitting the lottery. So, I say, take back control of your smile. Commit and sustain a concerted effort to place it on your face more often and for longer periods of time. It always pays to go the extra smile.

QUESTION FOR THE WEEK:
Am I smiling right now?

• BELIEVE IN YOURSELF •

When the adults in charge taught you as a child to trivialize and disparage your playful nature, it undermined your trust in your own intuition. It's about time you set things straight inside. Your natural self is uniquely gifted for success and happiness, and unleashing your humor nature will bring it forth in all its glory.

You are an original, not a copy. Never has there been anyone exactly like you and no one will ever be able to take your place. You've learned to treasure one-of-a-kind status in the "things" you collect and accumulate. Why not treasure a one-of-a-kind person—you?

Your humor nature believes in you deeply, just as you are. It knows all the dreams you dream and the hopes you hope. It knows you are a good person. It has this perspective on you simply because it resides in your heart, where even your so-called contradictions make perfect sense. It trusts you more than you trust yourself. Why not reciprocate?

Stop second-guessing yourself. You no longer need to be so fearful. The more in touch with your humor nature you become, the more confidently empowered you are.

The key to believing in yourself is to act like you do. When you feel doubt and uncertainty, act boldly on the faith that your humor nature will provide the answers. It won't let you down, and over time your confidence will grow. That's called "fake it until you make it." It works!

QUESTION FOR THE WEEK:
Am I acting as though I believe in myself?

• TELL THE TRUTH •

We've all heard it said that the truth will set you free. Be that as it may, I know this much. Telling the truth, even when it is painful, makes life a whole lot simpler. The truth stands on its own two feet. It doesn't need constant propping up or embellishment. Surrendering to your heart-based humor nature is a most reliable way to be consistently truthful. Your humor nature loves you too much to be party to a lie. So, in addition to providing you with lots of positive energy, your humor aptitude is both strengthened by the truth and a reliable way to keep yourself honest.

Humor and truth are intimately connected in many ways. A veteran comedian once told me he thought comedy was simply the simultaneous recognition of the absurdity of truth and the truth of absurdity.

Your humor nature assures you that the truth, no matter how painful it might be in the short run, is ultimately positive. That means whenever you speak negatively about yourself or someone else, you are not really telling the truth.

A principle function of humor is to make the truth more speakable and thus more bearable. "If you can laugh at it," comedian Bill Cosby says, "you can live with it."

QUESTION FOR THE WEEK:

Am I reflecting the positive truth in everything I say and do today?

• LISTEN VERY CAREFULLY •

I asked more than 100 performing comedians what they considered their most valuable skill in creating their comedy. The overwhelming majority gave the same answer: the ability to listen accurately. We usually miss most of the fun going on around us, simply because we are not listening carefully enough.

Last winter, I took a fall on some ice outside my office and hit my head hard on the sidewalk. Friends and colleagues who witnessed my fall *(nobody's ever around when I do something graceful)* insisted that I have the injury checked out at the University Hospital's Emergency Room. *(It wasn't the first time I'd been advised to have my head examined!)*

So, I went to the E.R. The intern on duty that morning was a recent graduate of our medical school, who seemed determined to impress his former professor (me) with his thoroughness. I received a complete work up, scores of x-rays, and even a pregnancy test (it was negative, in case you're wondering).

Presenting his findings to me, he proudly eliminated all of the "serious" possibilities, concluding with the following advice.

"Dr. Kuhn, the one thing we can't rule out is a subdural hematoma. So, you should be on the lookout over the next 36 hours for symptoms like nausea, dizziness, blurred vision, or drowsiness. As a matter of fact, just to be on the safe side, why don't you have your wife arouse you periodically through the night tonight."

Those were his exact words. He didn't hear them the way I did, but I was not about to let the opportunity pass.

"Could you write me a prescription for that? And put some refills on it, if you don't mind."

Even in the midst of serious events, listening carefully focuses you on the here and now, which is where all the fun is most likely to be found anyway.

QUESTION FOR THE WEEK:

Am I really listening to everything I'm hearing?

• LAUGH WITH YOURSELF •

The preposition is "with," not "at." Laughing *with* yourself is a true example of self-affirmation, one that will enable you to learn more quickly from your mistakes. It is a way of taking yourself lightly, while still taking your responsibilities seriously. Laughing with yourself opens up your creativity and makes you more resourceful. That's why you may have noticed that, when the going gets tough, the tough lighten up.

This exercise should help:

Sit quietly in a comfortable chair.

Take several deep, relaxing breaths. Try to release all of your tension as you let go of each breath. Dismiss all the usual thoughts from your mind and set aside, momentarily, any problems you have been wrestling with.

After approximately a dozen relaxing breaths, let your attention focus on a trait or characteristic of yours that you do not like. It can be physical, mental, or social. It doesn't matter. Just make sure it's something you don't like about yourself.

While keeping the "unwanted" trait in mind, try to think of a way this characteristic could be amusing. Be playful and gentle. Do not be unkind, sarcastic, or mean-spirited. Simply do what you can to see this trait in a more amusing or ridiculous light.

After a moment, discontinue this thought pattern and simply take a few more deep relaxing breaths. End the exercise by taking one final deep breath, slowly exhaling as you open your eyes, stretch your arms over your head, and then bring them back down to your sides.

QUESTION FOR THE WEEK:

How would I look or sound right now on Candid Camera?

• WELCOME YOUR MISTAKES •

If you are to rise above your fear and uncertainty, you must have the energy for it. Trying to deny your mistakes and keeping them hidden from others is a waste of precious energy.

Since you are perfectly imperfect, mistakes are inevitable. However, they can be real assets if you are willing to learn from them. Acknowledging mistakes freely is the first step in turning your perils into "pearls."

Mistakes teach you what doesn't work. Eliminating the wrong approach can be a step toward finding the right one.

Recognizing a mistake can often alert you to another point of view, or force you to develop new behaviors and coping styles, expanding your repertoire. The late *Tonight Show* host, Johnny Carson, was a master at deliberately making "mistakes" in his nightly monologue as a way of exercising his adlibbing skills.

One way to practice this strategy is to be like Johnny Carson. Make mistakes on purpose. Wear mismatched socks, or push the elevator button after it's already lit. I call this deliberate foolishness.

Deliberate foolishness will help you be more accepting of your mistakes. You'll get more used to feeling foolish, which can be exhilarating. You'll also discover that being deliberately foolish can be a marvelous stress reliever.

QUESTION FOR THE WEEK:

Am I getting the full benefit from the mistakes I'm making?

• CHALLENGE ALL ASSUMPTIONS •

Most of the fear you are experiencing right now relates to assumptions you have made based on past experience or the counsel of others (usually some form of hearsay). We all are tireless assumers, undeterred by ignorance of the facts. Whenever we don't know, we simply make more assumptions more quickly.

The problem is that most of these assumptions go unchecked, and before long, we treat them as facts and assign them the power of truth.

The problem is, most assumptions are wrong, and wrong assumptions can lead us a long way off course, when we're trying to be successful.

Challenging prevailing assumptions is standard operating procedure for all effective humor.

Develop the habit of playing *What If?* in your mind. Even if you are certain of your facts, *What If?* is still a good habit, because it will stimulate your creativity (eg. What if two plus two did not equal four?)

Practice playing *What If?* with common everyday objects. Look around the room right now and try it with anything you see. What if this pen was not a pen? What else could it be? A microphone ... a miniature space craft ... a jumbo tube of lipstick? What if this wasn't my hat? Would it be a Frisbee made of cloth ... a lunch box ... a potholder?

Resist any temptation to be funny with this strategy. There is no need for that. Simply allow your imagination to run free.

QUESTION FOR THE WEEK:

What if my assumptions about this situation are 180 degrees wrong?

• EXPECT THE UNEXPECTED •

As you were learning to be the overly serious person that you were before reading this book, you were bombarded with the notion that whatever you didn't know might hurt you. You were encouraged to look upon unexpected occurrences as signs of poor preparation or even incompetence. "I don't want any surprises" is the rallying cry of a fully prepared individual hoping for a successful mission.

It's important to unlearn that lesson. The unexpected will not hurt you. It will help you, if you let it, and it can be a pleasant experience, once you learn to turn it to your advantage. This strategy doesn't promote incompetence. It advocates flexibility. In a classic study of successful individuals it was found that those who showed the most resilience under stress shared the capacity to embrace unexpected occurrences as opportunities rather than setbacks. They seemed to "welcome" surprises and even to seek them out as stimuli to their growth and creativity.

The unexpected is the lifeblood of humor and fun. It encourages you to see different perspectives and points of view. It increases your awareness. That is the essence of growth, and growth is what you're here for.

Make it a practice to seek out surprises instead of avoiding them. Look carefully for the unexpected at all times, and even hope for it.

QUESTION FOR THE WEEK:
Who will surprise me today and how will it happen?

• LET GO FREQUENTLY •

Any experienced juggler will tell you that the secret to juggling success is not how many objects you can keep airborne simultaneously. Nor is it how high you can throw the objects in the air. It is how quickly you can let go of what is currently in your hand, so that you are able to catch what's coming next. What a great lesson for life. Letting go frees you to keep up with the flow.

Failure to let go of things increases your suffering and ineffectiveness. For instance, harboring a resentment, no matter how justified it might be, imprisons you while making no impact on the situation. It drains energy and limits your options. But, it's not easy to let go. The more important the issue, the harder it is to release your grip. This strategy asks only that you practice releasing what you can. Start with the easier things first. Don't let your major issues stand in the way of letting go of the smaller ones. Every little bit helps free you to be more resourceful and effective in your responses.

Wanda was despondent when her youngest child, Debbie, left home for college.

"It hit me harder than when the older ones left," she recalls. "I guess it was the realization that the nest was finally empty. I remember sitting in Debbie's bedroom and crying, as if she had died."

"It really helped when my friend Trudy invited me out to lunch," she continued. "We laughed over the silliest things and afterwards I noticed that I felt much better. More than at any other time I can remember, laughter helped me over the hump."

Your humor nature provides an effective and practically effortless way of letting go—laughter. You cannot laugh without letting go. Believe me. I tried that and it gave me a hernia.

You may find that, if you are able to let go, it will be only for a short time. Resentments and regrets have a way of building back up, with or without justification, and a renewed effort might be required tomorrow over the very same issue. If you keep at it, in time, it gets easier to loosen your grip and keep it loose.

QUESTION FOR THE WEEK:

What "extra baggage" am I carrying around with me today?

• STAY FOCUSED, BUT FLEXIBLE •

This sounds like an assignment for a contortionist. Focused and flexible? Aren't they opposites?

This strategy challenges you to keep your goals and priorities clearly in focus, while remaining flexible enough to accommodate the inevitable uninvited distractions.

Balance is the issue. If focus overrides flexibility, you become stubborn, rigid and bull-headed. If flexibility eclipses focus, you are aimless and vulnerable. Humor will help you avoid those extremes.

When it comes to flexibility, your humor nature offers you a so-called "win/win" situation. Flexibility stimulates your sense of humor, while humor in turn will keep you more flexible.

I find that personal humor "props" help me keep my focus and flexibility in balance. My favorite is my red sponge clown nose. Even before I put it on, if it's in my pocket, it helps me keep things in perspective. Believe me, no matter how serious the problem you may be facing, if you know you have a clown nose in your pocket or purse, you can't take yourself too seriously.

QUESTION FOR THE WEEK:
Where in my life has the intensity of my focus made me too inflexible?

• REACH OUT TO OTHERS •

We are not consistently capable of making the best decisions on our own. Reaching out to others helps create unbeatable synergy—the force that results from two or more people conjoining their energy. Of course this enhances the individual energies of everyone involved.

Another reason to reach out to others is that only by sharing your happiness can your joy be fully realized. As you experience a surge of happiness from reading this book, your first impulse is to share it and you should. It will open new doors to your existing relationships and extend your spirit into new circles of friendship.

And then there is the law of reciprocity. Your success is limited only by how successful you can help other people be. One sure way to receive the things you need is to focus on every opportunity to give those same things freely to those around you.

Thus, you open yourself up, not only to greater levels of energy and more happiness while reaching out to others, but also to additional help.

Bear in mind, this strategy calls for you to extend your reach beyond your current circle of friends and family. Get into the habit of striking up conversations during those common times of awkward silence, such as riding an elevator, sitting on a bus, or standing in line. The secret to reaching out at those times is to ask open-ended questions—questions that call for more than a "yes" or "no" answer. Make it an invitation for people to share a bit of themselves with you.

QUESTION FOR THE WEEK:

How can I express my genuine interest in the well being of others today?

• TAKE ACTION PROMPTLY •

As a student of relationship self-help books, Allison could tell her friends exactly what they should do to help their marriages. However, she had never put any of the same advice into action in her own life. Consequently, when she turned to me for help, she recited a long litany of romantic misfortune, including two failed marriages.

I denied her request for additional reading assignments, assuring her that she had absorbed more than enough information. It was time to get off the fence and move on the good advice she'd been dispensing to her friends.

I say much the same thing to you. You have hemmed and hawed long enough over missed opportunities and frustrated needs. I understand that you find a sense of comfort in taking no action. You can't fail if you don't try. In truth, the only real failure lies in not trying. It is far better to stub your toe as you learn how to ride your bike than to sit on the porch and preserve your pristine feet.

When you take action, you face two possibilities. Either you will achieve your goal or you won't. Which of the two possibilities will teach you the most? Usually you will learn more from a "failure." If that's true, is it accurate to use the word failure? So long as you learn from your miscue and endeavor not to repeat it, are you not a success?

QUESTION FOR THE WEEK:

What action am I putting off that could be as easily done right now?

• ADMIT WHEN YOU ARE WRONG •

My friend Lilly was never able to admit when she was wrong. Her reluctance to do so was distancing her from her husband and undermining what was once a beautiful relationship. Are you like Lilly? Chances are, if you are reluctant to admit mistakes, you are in the grip of an overly- serious perfectionism mindset. Perfectionism is the opposite of your true perfection. It is your attempt to be something you are not—an errorless, blemish-free person. Perfectionism is all about trying to measure up to imagined (and impossible) standards, so that others will accept you. And, most importantly, so you can accept yourself.

Unfortunately, nothing distances you from other people like perfectionism. Conversely, admitting when you are wrong builds bridges of trust between you and others. It portrays you as humble and self-confident.

When was the last time you actually said the words, "I was wrong?" Try saying them out loud right now: "I was wrong! You were right." Not that hard to say, is it? It gets easier with a little practice. And, when you say it to another person, you'll feel an uplifting infusion of energy that is released because you no longer need to maintain your illusions of perfection. You will be freed from the prison of your own unrealistically high expectations.

You'll get one other bonus. You'll discover that people aren't shocked and they really don't care that much. They're just grateful that you finally got around to it. You see, usually by the time you realize you are wrong, it has been obvious to everyone else for quite a while. You haven't really been fooling anybody but yourself, anyway.

Admitting when you are wrong takes courage and strength. In return for the effort, your friends will find you more worthy of trust. You'll be freed from the prison of your perfectionism, and you'll be infused with greater energy. In all, it's a great deal for saying just one little phrase.

QUESTION FOR THE WEEK:

Where have I been wrong and to whom can I admit it?

• DON'T LOOK DOWN •

A.J., the son of a good friend from California, is a surfer. To ride successfully, A.J. says, you must lose your sense of self, forgetting who and what you are in order to comingle your energy with that of the wave. "The minute you look down," he says, "and remember that you're a person balancing on a surfboard, you're toast."

A pretty good analogy for life, don't you think? You know when you're in the flow, when things feel like they're clicking and you don't have to wonder whether you're doing well. It just comes naturally. This smile strategy suggests that you look for that feeling daily and nurture it. When you use the power of your humor nature to reclaim your birthright of happiness, you're either effortlessly riding the wave or you're pretty darn close.

I know you don't like it when things aren't happening as you think they should or as fast as you'd like. You have neat and tidy plans that are constantly being rearranged by the force of the big wave you're riding. Still, I urge you not to look down.

When you look down, you're using your head. I want you to quit doing that so much. You're like the person who plants seeds in his garden, only to dig them up the next day to check their progress. There's a whole lot of life that you're not meant to figure out or control.

So, rely more on your heart, keep your eyes straight ahead, and have faith in what's going on below you. Sometimes the right hand doesn't need to know what the left hand is doing.

QUESTION FOR THE WEEK:
Am I thinking too much to enjoy the ride today?

• DON'T LOOK BACK •

Ruth had nine years of sobriety in Alcoholics Anonymous when she was diagnosed with lung cancer. She sought my help because she was having trouble dealing with her cancer. Having been a life-long smoker, she was blaming herself for bringing on the malignancy. Her self-condemnation was impeding her treatment as well as her peace of mind.

Having learned to let go of the past in her AA recovery work, Ruth found herself reverting to an old habit of looking at her life through a rear view mirror. Her preoccupation with regretting the past and feeling sorry for herself had re-awakened her urge to drink.

I think there's a little of Ruth in all of us. Whenever we look back, we hear the siren call of familiar pain. This smile strategy asks you not to waste time, energy and happiness by turning around to stare at the doors you've just closed. Your brain has an actual neural pathway burned into it for every habit you cultivate. Even after you jettison a bad habit, the neural paths remain, perhaps forever. Don't give them encouragement by lingering over what's past.

Instead, focus your attention on "burning" new neural pathways It may take a long time to make your new pathways more ingrained than the old ones you've been repeating for most of your life.

Don't be discouraged. You won't have to wait until all your old habits are replaced. Just don't give the past strength by dwelling on it. Turn around and face your bright new future.

QUESTION FOR THE WEEK:

Why am I wasting time and energy trying to redo what's already done?

• CELEBRATE EVERYTHING •

Perhaps you've heard the story of the optimistic little boy who, when confronted with a room full of horse manure, dove right in, exclaiming, "With all this manure, there's got to be a pony in here somewhere!" Although I wouldn't want to hug him right away, I think the little fellow's got it right.

No matter how big a pile of "manure" life may dump in your path, looking for the pony is the best response. When you opened your eyes this morning, you were already breathing. If not, I don't think you should be reading this.

If you went on to check the obituaries and didn't find your name listed, you're apparently alive. That's a miracle. Why not celebrate it?

Celebration is made up of two elements: gratitude and joy. Remember, joy is the most natural expression of your humor nature. If you want more joy in your life, begin each moment with gratitude.

Gratitude is the essence of celebration. It doesn't have to be noisy or raucous. A quiet "thank you" to a special person in your life can be an effective form of celebration. Another would be to deliberately listen for the sounds of laughter around you wherever you go.

QUESTION FOR THE WEEK:

Where will I find the pony in today's "manure?"

• KNOW THYSELF •

Knowing yourself well is the greatest safeguard against the encroachment of that dangerous enemy: your seriousness.

A self-inventory helps you sort out your actions and reactions, deciding if you are handling them to your liking or if you want to change what you're doing. One of the best things it does is help you separate your urgent tasks from your important ones.

An urgent task requires your immediate attention—your bank calling about a bounced check or a customer reporting she never received the merchandise she paid you for two weeks ago. You cannot ignore things like this or they will spread like wildfire. An important task is one which is easy to put off until tomorrow—reading a chapter of *Charlotte's Web* with your daughter or writing a letter to your old college roommate. These tasks will not bring your life to a halt if you don't address them today.

Why separate them? You don't want to overload your life with urgent tasks, because they'll burn you out faster than a sparkler on a hot July evening. Living a life dominated by urgent tasks is akin to running on a treadmill. You get really tired and you don't move an inch. Also preoccupation solely with urgent tasks leads to increased levels of seriousness and stress.

Knowing yourself puts you in touch with inner priorities, which will bring perspective to the urgencies raging on the outside. A personal inventory is not so much a "homework" assignment as it is a way of life.

QUESTIONS FOR THE WEEK:
What factors are compelling me today?
Am I being pushed or pulled?
What are my specific goals for today? Why?
What are my longer-range goals? What is my timetable?
How am I measuring my progress?
How is fun enriching my life today?

• SHARE THE LOAD •

Rose came to me complaining of low energy, depression, helplessness, and hopelessness. She was desperate for a solution. Already a successful businessperson with a thriving family of three children, she had all the trappings of success. She reported that she was doing a fine job of balancing her children's busy schedules, her husband's work hours, and her own job responsibilities, but she didn't know how much longer she could hold it together.

She was proud that up until recently she had been able to handle everything on her own, and embarrassed that she seemed to be slipping.

Like Rose, most people are shocked to discover how much freedom, energy and happiness they are losing by failing to delegate chores and responsibilities to others. Delegation may take more time initially, because you often have to teach people to do the tasks that you've been doing on their behalf. And then you have to trust that they will eventually do the job as well as you. But, the rewards far outweigh the up-front costs.

For one thing, sharing the load gives you the time and energy to take better care of yourself. For another, you will be amazed at how resourceful and talented others can be, once they know you're really counting on them. People tend to blossom right before your eyes when they realize that their roles are significant in your scheme of things.

QUESTION FOR THE WEEK:
What tasks can I let others do for me today?

• TURN IT OVER •

Fear, manifested through constant worry, was literally destroying Sophia's life. Divorced, she hadn't left her house, except to grocery shop, in over a year. She was almost to the point of giving up.

Sophia professed no faith in anything benevolent or guiding. She told me there was no God and, therefore, she was completely alone, at the mercy of whatever worst-case scenario her terrified imagination could come up with.

I told her the same thing I'm telling you now: Turn it over to someone else. You don't need to believe in my God, but you do need to find a power greater than yourself to which you can entrust the results of your efforts. This greater power can be any person, place or thing that can offer you reliable guidance and inspiration. You must trust the directions you get from this source and stop worrying about the outcomes. Turning things over means you quit worrying about them.

Once the reality of her limited options sunk in, Sophia took this smile strategy to heart. She decided to trust me initially. I suggested she attend a support group comprised of people who were successfully recovering from her dilemma. In time she "transferred" her trust to the collective wisdom of the support group. She was able to follow its guidance because she trusted the positive experiences reported by the members. What she received in return was a growing sense of serenity.

You can do the same. Do you remember being driven home by your parents, while you went to sleep in the back seat of the family car? What a secure feeling that was, knowing that a benevolent power greater than you was at the wheel. Nothing has changed. There's still a driver at the wheel. All you need to do is find who or what she is and turn it over to her.

Begin your search today. If you already have a power(s) greater than yourself in your life, redouble your efforts to turn over the results of your footwork. You deserve to ride safely home once more!

QUESTION FOR THE WEEK:

What higher power best serves my health and happiness today?

• LOCATE YOUR TARGET •

How pointless would it have been to rearrange the deck chairs on the Titanic? Would you take the time to carefully build a staircase that led up to ... nothing? Does preparing a sumptuous meal make sense before you know how many people will attend?

Of course these examples are ridiculous, but I'll bet you've done things just as absurd in your life. The point is even the best actions can be useless when you don't have a clearly defined goal in mind.

Establish short, medium, and long-term goals. Discover how much more fun it is, and how much more effective you become, when you align your actions with specific targets.

In fact, the very act of declaring your intended targets is often the catalyst that propels you toward reaching them. When you can see your target so clearly defined, it actually becomes difficult to veer off course.

Here's a three-step plan for setting up your target goals:

—Define at least three achievements you want to accomplish one year from now, five years from now, and ten years from now.

—For each desired outcome, create at least two action steps necessary to achieve it.

—Put the list in a place where you will encounter it every day. And read it every day. Start taking the action steps.

QUESTION FOR THE WEEK:
What short range or intermediate goal can I reach today?

• ASK AN EXPERT •

If you wanted to learn how to be a successful coach, would you seek the counsel of the guy whose team is in last place? If you needed a wilderness guide, would you hire someone who had never been camping before? If your goal were to accumulate great wealth, would you seek a mentor at the bankruptcy court?

The point is, as we've already observed, nobody achieves great health, happiness, or success entirely on his own. The Lone Ranger had Tonto, Batman had Robin, and Johnny Carson had Ed McMahon. If you are going to realize the full measure of your success, you will need a mentor.

Choose your mentor wisely. Don't ask the advice of someone who's likely to tell you what you want to hear. The true value of a mentor is in challenging you to grow past your present limitations. Comfort should not be your primary consideration. If you want commiseration, get a dog.

The mentor you seek should be a recognizable expert in the area you want to excel in and should want to help you succeed (You don't want a mentor who is interested in demonstrating his or her own expertise without advancing yours).

In life you're either growing or shrinking. If you wanted to shrink, you wouldn't be reading this. So, get out of your comfort zone and continue to grow.

QUESTION FOR THE WEEK:

Who can guide and push me to the next level, and how can I ask for her help?

• WHISPER SWEET NOTHINGS • IN YOUR OWN EAR

Begin practicing positive self-affirmations. Nothing is more important to your consistent happiness than what you say to yourself.

Perhaps you scoff at the notion of self-affirmations. Maybe you consider the practice a little too "new age." I have news for you. You're constantly saying things subconsciously to yourself already, but they might not be positive. Why not take charge of your internal script?

When I feel worried, I tell myself, "Everything is okay. I have everything I need and that will never change." Then, I force myself to believe what I've just told myself and to act as though I have that much courage and faith.

What happens? Most of the time I lose the fear and feel assured. Sometimes I will need to repeat the affirmation five minutes later, but so what? If I don't give myself the positive affirmation, it means I'm listening to the negative one that's making me worry. I get to choose what I tell myself!

Maria's big bugaboo was late night eating. She developed an affirmation telling herself that it was okay to go to sleep without a full belly. She has dropped four pounds and she's now using this strategy successfully in other areas of her life.

Why not follow Maria's example. Your internal monologue rages day and night, whether you take care to make it positive or not. Use this self-talk to build yourself up rather than tear yourself down.

QUESTION FOR THE WEEK:
Since I'm a good person, why shouldn't I get everything I need today?

• BELIEVE IT BEFORE YOU SEE IT •

"I'll believe that when I see it."

How many times have you said those words? Do you realize how completely backwards they are? According to the findings of quantum physics, you can now be certain that your beliefs directly impact your material world. In the most literal sense, you see things because you believe them—not the other way around. What you see when you open your eyes is very subjective and can be traced directly to what you believed you were going to see.

Does that mean if you believed there wasn't a wall in your bedroom, you could walk right through it? Let's not get carried away. What makes more practical sense is the notion that you can exert more control over shaping your beliefs by choosing what you surround yourself with. In turn your strengthened beliefs will influence the world you live and work in.

Here are some strategies:

—Create the world you wish to see inside your mind. Visualize people the way you'd prefer them to behave. Take care to think the best of all people and situations until they definitely prove otherwise.

—Surround yourself with positive things and people. Read uplifting books and listen to stirring music. Stop watching negative television or movies that reinforce old beliefs you've outgrown.

—Act courageously. It takes courage to act as if you believe something before you fully do. However, acting as though you believe the things you want to see, helps create the genuine belief systems necessary for you to exert more influence over your world. It is not an overnight process, but you will start to see changes as your beliefs really start to prevail.

—Don't be surprised when the beliefs you are now consciously choosing and nurturing manifest themselves right before your eyes. The energy and excitement you'll feel as you conjure this "magic," will rev up your humor nature. And your humor nature, in turn, will help you continue crafting new and positive beliefs.

QUESTION FOR THE WEEK:
What do I want to see happen today?

• TAKE CHARGE OF WHAT YOU CAN •

We've discussed many times your lack of control over the outcomes of your actions. True, I am a strong advocate of "letting go," but paradoxically there are a few things over which you exert absolute control and taking charge in those areas will help you just as much, if not more, than letting go in others.

You are always in control of your attitudes, your ideas and your actions. You are also the only person in the world capable of controlling them.

Carefully examine your attitudes and shape them into upbeat expressions of what you really believe. The same challenge holds for your ideas. Do not let negative ideas corrupt your thinking. They will drain you of your precious energy. Choose your actions carefully to conform to your attitudes and ideas.

QUESTION FOR THE WEEK:

What negative idea can I eliminate from my mind today?

• GIVE WHATEVER YOU WANT TO RECEIVE •

You get back in kind whatever you are willing to give freely. By practicing reciprocity you can actually choose, in a general way, the gifts you will get from life.

A patient, Donald, was very dedicated to increasing his income, so much so that he had become depressed over his lack of wealth-building progress. He had made the decision that real estate would be his ticket to riches, but he had received some bad advice and was losing money every month on his rental properties.

I received a despondent call. Donald had just heard from his property manager that he was going to go yet another month without any appreciable rental income. He was contemplating tossing everything and giving up. His brain was screaming, "Failure!" and he was shaken enough to want to retreat, clinging with both hands to what little money he had left.

I suggested to Donald that this might be a good time to engage the reciprocity principle. Since he wanted more money, I encouraged him to walk through his fear and commit to an act of courageous faith. I advised him in the midst of his economic woes to give away that which he wanted so badly. Fortunately for Donald, he was desperate enough to give it a try.

That same day he wrote a generous check to a worthwhile charity. Trusting the principle of reciprocity, he gave away the thing he wanted more of. He called me a week later to tell me about the sudden "appearance" of a reliable tenant for one of his most expensive properties, who had already paid the deposit and first month's rent in cash.

Coincidence? Nope. I've seen it happen too many times to write it off so trivially. Giving away what you desire really works. Donald is now a believer, and you will be too, if you try it.

QUESTION FOR THE WEEK:

Where can I give first the things I want to receive today?

• BE USEFUL •

What's your first reaction when you visualize a highly successful person? If you're like most people, you conjure images of moral and spiritual bankruptcy. That's understandable, because, from Ebenezer Scrooge to Bernie Ebbers, you are bombarded with the message that people of great success are greedy, lustful, mean and self-serving.

Nothing could be further from the truth. How do I know? I have been lucky enough to know more than a few highly successful people intimately. I have the private home phone number of one of the world's best-known celebrities. A gentleman whose personal net worth is in the hundreds of millions calls and writes regularly to seek my advice. I am a confidant and coach to the CEO of one of America's most successful corporations.

These individuals, and the many other successful people I'm fortunate to work and play with, share at least three traits: (a) Their success is real and lasting, extending well beyond mere monetary measurements; (b) They have lots of fun and are very happy; (c) They are among the most giving people I know.

It turns out that one of the hallmarks of great success is being useful in a way that helps others succeed as well. You hear so much about the Enrons of the world only because that sort of self-focused success is relatively fleeting.

Being useful works for at least three reasons. First, it is fun, inspiring and uplifting to help people and thus vicariously succeed through them. Second, you will always receive back in abundance that which you have given, so you will actually wind up benefiting much more than those whom you help. And, third, you are in no position to receive life's gifts until there is "space" for them in your life. By giving to benefit others, you open yourself up to receive.

For the greatest possible impact from this strategy, even though you know you will receive tenfold what you give, you must strive to be useful without expecting a specific return. Have no agenda but to help others succeed. Even before you begin "receiving back," you'll be having more fun along the way.

QUESTION FOR THE WEEK:
How can I be most useful to someone else today?

• SHARPEN YOUR AXE •

Abraham Lincoln was reported to have said, "If you give me three hours to chop down a tree, I'll spend the first two sharpening my axe."You may agree with his approach, but I'll bet you don't dedicate that percentage of time to your personal preparation for life.

Your mind, spirit, and body are crying out to be taken care of, and ignoring this discipline is making you much more unhappy than you need to be.

You wouldn't wait until your entire roof caves in before replacing a few leaky shingles, would you? Yet, you take the very same risks with your own well-being. You wait until you are lonely, depressed, or ill before making a greater effort to care for yourself.

Here's how to begin "sharpening your axe" today:

—Choose a method of physical renewal. Unless you're already exercising regularly, I suggest walking for 30 minutes three or four times per week.

—Choose a method of mental renewal. Reading an exciting, motivating, and/or inspiring book for 20 or 30 minutes before bed each night might be a good place to start.

—Choose a method of spiritual renewal. This could be as simple as sitting quietly in a tranquil place for 10 or 15 minutes. Don't overlook the fact that laughing can be good for your spirit, as well as your body.

QUESTION FOR THE WEEK:

What can I do today to maintain the "sharpness" of my physical, mental, and spiritual tools?

• FIND THE RAY OF HOPE •

German psychiatrist, Viktor Frankl, watched his wife, parents and brother perish in Nazi concentration camps during World War II. In the midst of daily torture and deprivation, Frankl realized that he alone had control over his responses. He began to look for a ray of hope in these dark events, by imagining himself, after being freed, having the chance to teach his patients this survival skill.

In time, Frankl realized that he was actually freer than his Nazi captors, because he was in control of his responses, while theirs dominated them. In fact, so great did his light shine after he learned to start looking for the ray of hope, that many of the camp guards began to admire Dr. Frankl, asking him for advice and counsel.

You've learned in this book that even a "fake" smile introduces physiological and psychological benefits that will soon have you feeling good enough to support a genuine one. Looking for the ray of hope in every dark cloud does the same thing. You are guaranteed to be happier, whether you find it or not, because the act of looking introduces beneficial biological and emotional results.

QUESTION FOR THE WEEK:

What possible benefits will I discover in today's "dark cloud?"

• SIT STILL •

"Arrgh!" I yelled, red-faced with anger. I was tearing apart my hotel room looking for my car keys. It was already eight minutes past checkout time and in another five minutes I would be late for my sendoff speech at the Association for Applied and Therapeutic Humor's annual meeting.

In desperation I sat down on the bed, trying to remember the last place I had seen the keys. From my vantage point I could see outside the window a gorgeous cumulus nimbus cloud framed against a picture-perfect azure morning sky. For the first time since my rampage had begun, I relaxed and thought about how fortunate I was to catch that beautiful sight. I even had a brief whisper of gratitude.

As I looked down from the cloud, there were my car keys, sitting on the window ledge, where, of course, they had been all along. My frustration and anger had literally blinded me.

It's amazing how quickly we can lose sight of what's important or even real, isn't it? If you take time each day to just sit, the payoff will be greater awareness, lower frustration, and more fun. Good deal, huh?

A method for sitting still:

Begin by removing yourself from your immediate concerns. If you are carrying out a responsibility that won't permit your physical removal, you can simply close your eyes and, as much as possible, block outside stimuli.

Find a beautiful or joyful image or sound on which to focus. It's okay to use a memory of something beautiful.

Concentrate completely on that image or sound. Take in the awesome miracle of life it represents, which you might usually take for granted. Marvel at its perfection.

Listen to your image and sound with both your heart and your ears. It has something to communicate to you, and, if you sit still enough, you'll be amazed at the message it reveals.

The exercise just described makes a wonderful meditation, lasting as long as you desire. However, it works just as well if used during a three-minute break. Do you have three minutes to spare today, in return for supercharged energy, focus and happiness?

QUESTION FOR THE WEEK:
What am I overlooking because I'm not sitting still?

• GIVE PEOPLE WHAT THEY NEED •

Researchers tell us that our highest need, after basic biological necessities are satisfied, is to be accepted and understood. You can fulfill this need for others by giving them your full attention, which involves active listening. Active listening means listening empathically, with all your senses. It takes your full concentration, since more than 80% of all communication is nonverbal.

Active listening gives people the acceptance they need to feel validated and valued. It inspires trust and openness, which are the fertile breeding grounds for fun and fulfilling human interactions.

You are not merely trying to understand the meaning of the words people are using, but also the thoughts and emotions behind them. Ask questions instead of making statements. Don't be in such a hurry to give advice. Seek to understand the other person's point of view more fully.

QUESTION FOR THE WEEK:
What is in the way of my giving this person my undivided attention?

• KEEP YOUR HANDS EMPTY •

A successful CEO, Felicia had earned the respect of her male counterparts by beating them at their own game—outworking them. It was exhausting to spend time with her, because she never stopped. She was constantly "on the clock." Even her social activities were driven by her business objectives.

Something had to give, and in this case it was Felicia's health. Cancer reared its fearsome head and forced her to the sidelines. As you might expect, she was at first infuriated and then depressed. However as she endured the extended recuperation from her surgery, and became encouraged by her survival odds, she confessed to me that her "down time" was permitting her to rediscover some things she had enjoyed in her earlier life, but had eliminated in favor of her career: things like music, detective novels, movies and sunsets—"the expendable stuff."

"I had forgotten how much I enjoyed those things," she said. "I don't intend to get that busy again. It's not worth it." I hope she sticks to that promise and you follow her lead.

The best way to continue receiving more of what brings you joy is to continually empty your hands of the things you already have. Share out of your abundance and try to keep your hands empty. You will soon discover that more of what you wanted was only waiting for you to become "free" to receive it. After all, you can't "freshen up" a cup of coffee that is already filled to the brim.

QUESTION FOR THE WEEK:

Am I already too "full" to receive the gifts that await me today?

• SEE THE WORLD THROUGH • THE EYES OF A CHILD

When did your childlike curiosity die? When did you lose the ability to marvel at the elegant complexity of our world? It happened to most of my patients when they decided to grow up, become serious, and have all the answers. At that point, childlikeness "became" childishness, a trait that got in the way of responsible adult behavior.

Being childlike is vital to your lasting health and success.

I took my nine-year-old grandson to the state fair last summer, with an ambitious agenda in mind for hitting all the sights. We started with the farm animal wing and he found it so fascinating he didn't want to leave. I got frustrated by his "dallying" and insisted that we move on.

As we marched through the fair to our next destination, I noticed that his smile was gone, as was his enthusiasm. I suddenly realized that I had trampled on his natural curiosity in order to serve my adult agenda.

We did an immediate about face. I started paying attention to my grandson's fascination. I never had so much fun looking at cows, pigs, sheep and goats, because I was seeing them as if for the first time. I was seeing them through his eyes.

You can adopt a child's point of view any time you choose and no child need be present. However, I suggest you recruit a child to come along whenever you can. She will have a ball as she unknowingly mentors you, reacquainting you with childlikeness. Engrave her teachings into your brain.

QUESTION FOR THE WEEK:

How would a nine-year-old child see this situation?

• STAND ON YOUR HEAD •

"You don't know anything about this ... and you don't care how I feel!" yelled my teenage daughter. I was on the receiving end of a typical my-father-is-an-idiot teenage diatribe, circa 1987. Isn't it amazing how stupid you become when your children hit puberty?

Guess what I did.

I started to chuckle. My daughter, recognizing that the laughter wasn't aimed at her, couldn't resist smiling at my big goofy grin. "What's so funny?" she asked.

What, indeed! I had just discovered a secret method for

having fun in almost any situation. Stand on your head! Use your imagination to flip the world upside down and reverse roles.

What made me chuckle that day was the appearance, out of the blue, of an absurd image in my mind's eye: my daughter as my mother and me as her son. This placed the subject matter of my daughter's protests in a ridiculous juxtaposition with my upside down image and spawned a goofy grin.

Of course, in many situations you might not want to express outward laughter. The traffic cop who pulls you over for speeding might not appreciate it. But, you don't need to laugh out loud for this powerful strategy to work.

In fact, I recommend you stick with private enjoyment of your upside-downing, because most of the situations in which you'll find it useful will probably be potentially contentious. By standing on your head, you're eliminating the stress that might otherwise disable you.

QUESTION FOR THE WEEK:

What would this situation look like upside down or reversed?

• ASK THE DUMB QUESTION •

Mark Twain once said, "Better to keep your mouth closed and be thought a fool than to open it and remove all doubt." He was an amazing man, but I think he got that one wrong. There really are no dumb questions.

Curiosity is the lifeblood of your humor nature. You have a responsibility to nourish it and that sometimes requires asking a "dumb" question. Besides, you know as well as I do that, when someone finally asks that kind of question, you say to yourself, "I'm sure glad he asked that." Once your ego is out of the way, you're full of questions, just as you were as a child.

Ask every question as it occurs to you. If somebody really does think your question is dumb, that's a person to avoid anyway.

QUESTION FOR THE WEEK:
What do I want to know that I'm afraid to ask about?

• SAY WHAT EVERYBODY ELSE IS THINKING •

My patient, Evan, was disabled and in chronic pain. His wife, Marcy, was his primary caregiver. The two had suffered a very hurtful blow-up, and Marcy had announced that the damage to their marriage was in her opinion irreparable. The three of us were meeting in my office at my request.

You could have hung cold cuts in the chilled atmosphere. I tried to get Marcy and Evan talking, but the silence was deafening. I took another approach.

"Marcy," I said, "you think I'm on Evan's side because he's my patient, don't you? I don't blame you. Why don't you tell me how you feel about me and my relationship with Evan?"

You'd have thought Mount St. Helens had erupted right there in my treatment room. She politely, but definitely, laid out her concerns and laid into me. How dare I presume to know enough to judge their relationship, based solely on my conversations with Evan?

Did we all hold hands and sing "Kumbaya" from then on? Heck no. But once Marcy got that off her chest and had some of her fears put to rest, the two began to talk in earnest about their relationship. I'm happy to report they are still together—a definite work in progress, but still married.

Many times an impasse or stalemate occurs in human relationships because no one is willing to name the elephant that everyone knows is sitting in the room. If you want to keep your relationships vital, you must at times be willing to say what everyone else is thinking. Even if no one agrees with your assessment, "naming the elephant" gives everyone permission to talk about it.

Tell people frankly what you think. Express what you're observing. Share what you feel. Do it with love, compassion, and, where possible, gentle humor and it won't matter whether or not you are correct. You'll be helping your friends and family by opening a door for sharing and honest interaction.

QUESTION FOR THE WEEK:

How can I help overcome the fear of the obvious today?

• START WITH YOUR HEART •

My wife, Connie, is one of the most youthful, energetic, and healthy people I know. Want to know her secret? It's simple. Connie always starts with her heart. Leading with her heart, she finds joy in almost everything she does.

The simplest way to start with your heart is to create an internal rule: all people and experiences in life are useful, positive, and good until proven beyond a doubt to be otherwise. This means you open yourself to people and experiences with minimal prejudgment.

At the same time it is important to protect yourself when you find a person or experience unworthy of your trust by distancing yourself from that person or experience. Summon the courage to be vulnerable and childlike for an entire day of starting with your heart.

QUESTION FOR THE WEEK:

Am I keeping my heart open to new people and experiences today?

• GET OUT OF YOUR MIND •

In the early days of psychiatric practice, patients who sought my help seemed obsessed with the question,"Why do I behave the way I do?" Dutifully I would try to help them examine their family life, childhood, ancestry, school experiences, dreams, peer relationships, and anything else that might offer a clue—all in an attempt to answer,"Why?"

I have learned over the years that trying to figure out why you do something is about as useful to your happiness as roller skates on a pig. That's because it's almost exclusively about using your head.

To affect real change you must leave the limited confines of your mind and your thoughts and stop analyzing.

It's time to get out of your mind and take action today. I'm not advocating impetuous and thoughtless action, but if that were your only alternative to staying in your head, I'd rather see you become impetuous. That's how important it is to get out of your mind.

You can continue to seek sage advice (you're reading this book, aren't you?), make plans and test the depth of the water before diving in. But then, get out of your mind. Sure you're going to make some mistakes, but not as many as you think. When someone says, "You must be out of your mind." You can reply, "Yes I am. Thank you for noticing."

QUESTION FOR THE WEEK:

How can I get out of my head without losing my mind?

• TAKE THE LONG VIEW •

We all suffer from exaggerating the importance of whatever is currently on our plates: admission to college, a presentation at work, preparing for a dinner party. It's natural for things to appear much more dire when they are urgent, pressing and in your face.

Whenever this happens, try asking yourself, "What difference will this make in ten years?" Very few of your worries will stand up to that test.

Try it right now. What is your most pressing worry? Your dissertation defense next Thursday? Your mother-in-law's disapproval of your vacation to Disney World? The teenager down the street who plays his rap music loud enough to rattle your fillings?

If you could meet yourself ten years from now, your future self would kick your present-day butt for allowing one moment of this beautiful day to be taken up by these trivial worries. Follow your future self's sage advice. Take the long view and don't sweat the small stuff.

QUESTION FOR THE WEEK:
What differences will any of this make in ten years?

• BE CONSTANTLY CURIOUS •

I was a curious youngster. Growing up outside Philadelphia, Pennsylvania, I loved the Phillies professional baseball team. My favorite player was their star pitcher, Hall-of-Famer, Robin Roberts. I used to wonder what would happen if I just showed up on his doorstep one day to talk to him.

So, that's what I did. One day, my brother, Doug, and I looked up his address and rode our bikes to his house. We didn't know any better, but we had no malicious intent. Of course, this was a more innocent time, so I'm happy to report that my hero welcomed us, talked with us for a while, and even autographed our baseball mitts (for free!). My curiosity was satisfied.

Stripped of self-serving motivation, curiosity will always open doors and provide ample opportunities for fun.

You might practice your curiosity at work. What will happen if you decide to greet every co-worker and customer this week with the friendliest smile you've got? How about a decision to answer the phone all week with,"Hello. How can I make you happy today?"You can satisfy your curiosity by trying these things.

Or, you may decide to apply your curiosity at home. What would happen if, at dinner tonight, you asked each family member, "What was the most fun thing you did today?" A wonderful benefit of being constantly curious is that you remain more receptive to new information. Nothing feeds "steroids" to your humor nature quite as fast as new information being pumped into a curious brain.

QUESTION FOR THE WEEK:
What's under this rock?

• BE PLAYFUL •

No matter what your circumstances are, taking yourself lightly makes you more creative, resourceful, adaptive, responsive, and resilient. But, how do you remain playful at all times? Good question, because there are many occasions where laughter and joking are not appropriate. It's important to remember that your playfulness need not always be expressed externally.

The best way to implement this strategy is to turn tasks into games. Playing with words you hear or read is another option. Playing with time is still another.

Here's how my son Greg has used being playful to stay healthy and successful at his work. Greg is a high school assistant principal, a disciplinarian, and there are many occasions, such as field trips, dances, and pep rallies, when Greg is called upon to supervise large groups of rambunctious teenagers. Refusing to become a mean "hockey goon" and wear a scowl, Greg makes a game out of it.

Sometimes he pretends to be James Bond, looking for dangerous international spies in the large crowd he's chaperoning. At other times Greg pretends he is a shark swimming alongside schools of tuna. These games are always private (until now). All anyone else sees is Greg doing a great job supervising and disciplining teenagers. Who would imagine Greg is actually having fun in a potentially high stress situation?

QUESTION FOR THE WEEK:
What kind of game would make this task more fun?

• EXAGGERATE AND MINIMIZE •

Joke-writers know that by stretching or shrinking any concept to the extremes, they can find humor. But, you don't have to be a comedy professional to benefit from this phenomenon.

When I discovered she was living nearby, I was very excited about the possibility of collaborating with the woman who invented solitaire. I've always loved solitaire and enjoyed discovering new variations over the years. I thought she and I would make a good team.

But she wouldn't even consider it. She told me, "I work alone!" I should have seen that coming.

Did that exaggeration of reality make you smile? That's what this smile strategy is all about. Even if you don't laugh out loud, stretching or shrinking the meaning of words or ideas engages your healthy humor nature.

Exaggerating and minimizing words can keep you constantly entertained. With the English language at your disposal, you have so many double meanings to work with.

Knock, knock. Who's there? Dewey. Dewey who? Dewey have to listen to these jokes all night?

Exaggerating and minimizing puts you more in charge of your options in every circumstance. Whether or not you share your silliness with anyone else is entirely up to you.

QUESTION FOR THE WEEK:
Would it help to exaggerate or minimize how I feel right now?

• ENJOY THE GAME •

Do you think life is all about arriving at a destination, rather than making the most of the journey? Focusing on results divorces you even further from the process and the moment. Therein lies the problem, because the process is where you experience your growth, while the moment is where you find all your fun.

You can ill afford to shortchange yourself in those two areas.

By enjoying the game, you will gradually dispel the myth that happiness awaits you once you buy that dream home, receive that promotion, pack the children off to college, or at long last retire. Take a moment to savor instead what you like most about where you are presently living, the satisfaction you derive from your job, the small daily pleasures your children give you. You will discover instead that your happiness is "awaiting" you right here and right now.

QUESTION FOR THE WEEK:
If I'm already having fun, what do I care about keeping score?

• CHOOSE PROGRESS OVER PERFECTION •

Refusing to accept yourself—to love yourself—until certain conditions are met is a fear-based strategy. Fear-based energy is only good for occasional emergency situations. Over the long haul, it will burn you out quicker than a stair-stepper set on level 9, leaving you feeling that: (a) You haven't accomplished your goal; (b) you're burnt out; and (c) you're beating yourself up for failing, yet again.

Choosing progress over perfection allows you to jettison your unrealistic expectations and comparisons. You are, after all, exactly where you're supposed to be and comparing your insides to other people's outsides is a losing game.

Accept that your foibles and shortcomings—those parts of you for which you so often beat yourself up—are just as essential to your humanity as your more agreeable characteristics. The goal is not to rid yourself of your inconsistencies and mistakes. It is rather to learn from them and grow. This is the essence of progress and it is all you'll ever need to be happier and healthier every day.

QUESTION FOR THE WEEK:
What if I am really a good person already?

• AGREE TO DISAGREE •

In 1976, Tom, my best friend from the Air Force, moved to Louisville, close to my current home. I knew Tom had cancer, but I didn't know he had given up and was coming to Louisville to die. When he shared this with me, I thought he was foolish for giving up and fought with him about it.

My attempts to change Tom's mind failed. But, I couldn't let go of my anger over his self-serving decision. After all, I knew alternative and adjunctive treatments I could introduce him to. In my anger, I washed my hands of him and walked away.

Seven months later, Tom died. After learning of his death, I knew I had made a bad mistake. My inflexibility had cheated me out of precious time with my friend.

Other people will not always see things the way you do and neither of you will be able to persuade the other to change. In order to avoid shutting yourself off from the energy and love you need from important relationships, it is necessary to agree to disagree.

Two things happen when you practice this strategy. First, you affirm your respect for the other person. Second, you retain your own openness and the positive energy you receive from the relationship will continue to flow. You don't stop loving somebody, just because you disagree with him wholeheartedly.

Doesn't it sound healthier to have more communication in your life?

QUESTION FOR THE WEEK:
Is it really that important to have everyone agreeing with me today?

• OCCASIONALLY BOOK • THE TOUGH ROOMS

Comedians call unreceptive or unappreciative audiences "tough rooms." Playing tough rooms can sometimes feel like taking a dose of bitter medicine, but what a powerful medicine it can be. And, as with medicine, the bitter taste is only temporary.

How do you play the tough rooms in your day-to-day life? You start simply by making a commitment not to shirk, or duck out on, difficult people or challenges that cross your path.

The keys to making the most of the "tough room" experience are:

—Practice patience, mostly with yourself. You will probably not "perform" as well as usual in a tougher situation, so give yourself some latitude for mistakes.

—Enjoy the experience. As you know, the lessons don't come from your results. You learn from the process. The muscle flexing at the end of a workout is not what builds you body. It's the grunting and groaning you just put into lifting those weights.

—Keep your eye on the prize. While the "audience" in your tough room will likely forget your performance, you can benefit for a lifetime from the new tools and skills you'll learn.

—The long-term benefits of playing the tough rooms, when they arise, are a sharpened humor nature and a keener sense of fun.

QUESTION FOR THE WEEK:

What have I got to lose by playing this "tough room?"

• EAT YOUR BRUSSELS SPROUTS FIRST •

We all put off unpleasant duties, but procrastination can keep you up at night worrying and disable your humor nature. That's why it's important to do your most unpleasant tasks first and get them over with.

Do you know what a great feeling it is to be free of that thing you've "been meaning to do?" Imagine feeling that kind of exuberant freedom anytime you choose. Eat your brussels sprouts first!

I love public speaking, but every time I do it I feel a small gnawing fear of strangers in the audience. Earlier in my speaking career, I simply talked myself out of the fear and went full steam ahead. I've learned a better way and it's a form of eating my brussels sprouts first. As soon as I arrive at the event, I go into the crowd and meet as many people as I can.

Perhaps I've met you this way. You just thought I was a nice guy (which I am). You didn't know I was eating my sprouts. But, your warm handshake, bright smile and kind words of greeting were just what I needed to feel like I was no longer amongst strangers. I'm a better speaker when I'm among friends.

QUESTION FOR THE WEEK:
What can I do to put this uninviting task behind me?

• EMBRACE YOUR DEFEATS •

Defeats are a natural by-product of living fully., In a famous speech given at the Sorbonne in Paris, France, on April 23, 1910, Teddy Roosevelt said: "... The credit belongs to the man who is actually in the arena, whose face is marred by dust and sweat and blood; who strives valiantly; who errs, who comes short again and again, because there is no effort without error and shortcoming ..." This is the way successful people regard their defeats.

What is a defeat, really? It is an unplanned and often unwelcome outcome—a knee-bending curveball thrown when you are expecting a big fat fastball over the heart of the plate. You've been taught to hate the unexpected outcomes we call defeats.

What is a joke, really? It is an unplanned and often unwelcome (at least when I'm telling one) outcome—a missing step that sends you into a pratfall when you are expecting one to be there. You've been taught to love the unexpected outcomes we call jokes.

Why do you love one and hate the other, when, in principle, they're the same thing? Well, from now on, you don't have to practice this dichotomy. You can take your love of humor and apply it to your defeats. Look out world. Here you come.

We are talking about embracing defeats, not failure. There's a difference. A defeat is normal and inevitable, while failure is not. Failure only becomes real if you quit. Usually, it's accumulated unembraced defeats that motivate you to quit. So, by embracing your defeats, you're actually taking out insurance against failure.

QUESTION FOR THE WEEK:
What can I learn from my defeats today that will move me closer to success?

• CONDUCT A LAUGHTER SYMPHONY •

What is a laughter symphony? Quite simply it is the sound of joy that is abundantly produced around you during every moment of your day. You already know there are "stages" of laughter to listen for. But, you don't have to restrict yourself to that. Joy can be heard in something as delicate as a cheerful inflection in someone's voice. It can be seen in something as unobtrusive as a tiny grin on a beaming face.

Joy is everywhere.

Before you balk at the simplicity of this smile strategy, allow me to call attention to something that clearly illustrates its potential value to you.

Laugh tracks are a staple of television sitcoms. They are at best annoying; at worst, downright insulting. So, why do the studios continue to use them? Because, they work!

Laugh tracks tap into a preconditioned psychological trigger that you share with all other humans. The trigger is that you take behavioral cues from the actions of other people around you. If you hear an audience laughing, it makes you think the show is funny. You are not stupid, but rest assured this trigger has a deep subconscious effect on you , just like all of us. That's why TV executives continue to serve up laugh tracks.

Think of the ramifications. You can use this subconscious trigger to your own advantage any time you wish. The laughter symphony around you can become your personal "laugh track."

What are the benefits? If you are like my patients, you'll be smiling twice as often, laughing more regularly and have 60% more energy and a third less physical pain. These are only averages, mind you. You may do much better.

QUESTION FOR THE WEEK:

What kind of concert will the laughter symphony play for me today?

• GET LOST •

When I was a teenager, I sought the counsel of a wise guru. I told him I was just trying to find myself. He told me to get lost.

Now I know what he meant. I watch a young child at play. I see how utterly absorbed she is with her game. It's pure immersion. She is not conscious of being a child. She has lost herself completely in the moment.

You were born with that same ability to lose yourself. You have not lost it. It remains one of your greatest gifts, because it puts you in the present moment, where all the fun is.

Legendary comedian Chris Rush told me there are three things that root us in the moment as adults: great sex, gunfire, and laughter. I'll add one more: your decision to surrender completely to the moment. You can cultivate the capacity to get lost.

Right now you are spending far too much of your time and mental energy absorbed by two illusions that weigh you down like anchors tied to your neck in the deep end of the pool. They are setting goals for the future and remembering the past. Come on. That doesn't require 96% of your life. Save some time for right now.

How do you keep your focus on the here and now as much as possible? By trying to immerse yourself completely in whatever you are doing. Whether you're driving to the grocery, raking leaves in your yard, or making a ham sandwich, be there in that moment.

And when someone tells you to, "Get lost," reply, "Thanks for the reminder."

QUESTION FOR THE WEEK:
Where can I lose myself today?

• BECOME A PROP MASTER •

Would a competent director stage a theatrical production without props? Of course not. Props add to the power of the performers to influence the attitude of the audience. So, why would you "stage" your day without humor props to positively influence yourself and those around you?

A humor prop is anything that brings a smile, banishes your seriousness, lifts your mood, or reminds you to take yourself lightly. If you make a commitment to become a humor prop master and surround yourself with humor props, you will find yourself with fewer negative attitudes.

Some of my favorite humor props include funny calendars, socks, ties, underwear, emails and cartoons. Above all I keep a clown nose with me constantly. I don't wear it all the time, but it's always in my pocket, reminding me to stop taking slow traffic, jammed copy machines, and credit card bills so seriously.

Humor props don't have to be funny, expensive, or even visible to anyone else. They are just for you, inspiring you to lighten up and get back on the road to success through fun and humor.

QUESTION FOR THE WEEK:
Should I share my humor prop or keep it to myself right now?

• ACCEPT THE THINGS YOU • CANNOT CHANGE

When you accept something, you don't automatically like it, endorse it, or even agree with it. You just stop fighting it. Your humor nature will help you stop fighting the battles you can't win. Of course, you won't think of smiling when someone cuts you off in traffic or when your daughter sneaks out to attend a forbidden party. But if you notice the humor in your reaction, it will help.

You can find the humor in your mistaken assumption that you have control over such things. You don't have control and you never did. It was an illusion.

Watching a child reach up to grab the object appearing "right before her eyes" during a 3-D movie makes you laugh gently because it's sweet and cute. Why is your attempt to grasp your illusion any less humorous (and any less sweet and cute)? The answer is, it's not.

The more you practice finding the humor in your illusions of control, the easier time you will have accepting what you cannot change. It's a wonderful reciprocal relationship, because accepting the things you can't control, in turn, makes it easier to find the humor.

You'll soon realize that, by giving in, you're not giving up anything except the things you never had anyway.

QUESTION FOR THE WEEK:

Why should I waste energy fighting battles I've already lost?

• KEEP YOUR STEREOTYPES IN CHECK •

When you were a child you knew nothing of categories and stereotypes. You viewed every encounter and experience as though it were for the first time, because usually it was. Everything stimulated your curiosity. Everything was exciting. And everything was more fun.

As you matured, you were taught to categorize and label your experiences. Having a name for something made it more familiar and predictable, and usually less exciting. We've all heard the dismissive phrase, "Been there; done that!"

Now, in adulthood, you have amassed a huge inventory of categories and stereotypes that enable you to draw on past experiences to more efficiently deal with the challenges you face each day. You would never think of taking on life without resorting to the benefit of your accumulated experience. In this way stereotyping makes you more efficient. I'm not suggesting there is anything wrong with that. If you had to start from scratch each time, you wouldn't get much done.

I am suggesting, however, that anything that increases your efficiency can improve your life if used as a tool in your hand, but can also ruin it if given unchecked dominance. If stereotyped thinking dominates you to the point that it interferes with your ability to focus on the present moment and to learn from the unique and personal elements of each encounter, it will compromise your health and success.

This smile strategy provides you with a safeguard against that risk, by encouraging you to keep your efficiency, but not let it cut you off from the "miracles" occurring in your life. It recommends that you frequently look at everything with fresh eyes.

I think you can guess what awaits you when you do this. Your humor nature will show you a lot of fun that you've been missing by relying on outdated stereotypes.

QUESTION FOR THE WEEK:

Am I using my experience or is it using me?

Step Six: Do Something...Now!

"Action reduces the lion of terror to an ant of equanimity."
—Og Mandino, author of The Greatest Salesman in the World

They say he who hesitates is lost.

In the first place, I don't know who they are. And, what's more, I don't agree with them.

To my way of thinking, he who hesitates is not lost at all. He knows exactly where he is, and so does everybody else. He's stuck in the starting gate. Moreover, we all know what he's doing: choking on the dust of others.

I think "they" should say he who hesitates has lost, or soon will. That would be closer to the truth.

I have a friend who has a wonderful idea for a business. Everyone tells her it's a concept that can't miss. She has developed a business plan that draws rave reviews from her colleagues and supporters. She even has created signage and a layout for her business site. She talks about his idea with every person who will sit still long enough to listen. She has accumulated an impressive "board" of trusted advisors and legions of well-wishers.

In short, she has done everything a person must do to be successful. She lacks only one thing. She hasn't taken action. She continues to wait for just "the right moment." By now it has been years since she first articulated her vision. Those of us who know her best have begun to doubt that she will ever take "the plunge."

That's the way it is with action. You can dream and even talk a "good game," but that's no substitute for real action. Taking action can be daunting. Yet nothing really makes a difference until you do. Life itself is action. It is not a "spectator sport." Life is to be lived and living involves exposing yourself to a certain degree of uncertainty. It is at times unpredictable and always unmanageable, which is why it can be tempting to remain an armchair theorist, instead of a practical "doer."

Up until this point, I've allowed you to sit in that armchair. I've asked you to shift your attitude towards humor and challenged you to surrender to your personal humor aptitude. As important as those changes are, they involved little risk and no real "irreversible" consequences.

Now we move to the third "HA" of our HA HA HA Prescription: *Humor Action.*

Humor action is any tactic or behavior that you employ to increase the fun in your environment and give your humor nature maximum opportunity to prevail. Humor action makes a tangible positive impact on any situation. It's a way for you to constantly "seed the solution." You know now that humor lurks beneath everything in life and will eventually emerge, if given enough time. Your humor actions will speed up the emergence process, so you can enjoy more fun sooner.

For example, every time I get in an elevator with other people, I find it amusing that we all automatically face forward and stare at the numbers. Allowing my mind to privately play with this observation does me some good, but if I take action on it, I can multiply the potential benefits to myself, and the others in the car as well. So, I move to the front of the car, turn and face everyone else. Then I say, "If I had known there would be so many of us, I would have scheduled this meeting in a larger room. Has anyone read over the minutes from our last meeting? I'll entertain a motion to approve them as circulated..."

Well, you get the picture. Yes, it's a little risky, but do you know what happens most of the time? People jump right into the playfulness. Someone offers to record the minutes. Others nominate officers. By the time we've gone a few floors, we are having so much silly fun that people are almost reluctant to get off the car. If someone new gets on, we inform her that we started the meeting without her and elected her president. It's as if everyone was just waiting for the opportunity to be playful. It figures, since our humor natures are always looking for an outlet.

Whenever you initiate a humor action, you will find the same thing to be true. With rare exception, people are eager to join in. It's important to remember this, because let's admit it, for most of us action is difficult. As we said, it usually involves risks and consequences.

The challenge of this step is to turn the positive energy you've generated from your revitalized attitude and aptitude into a life of positive action. It's time to move past the "safety" of the armchair and dive into the action. It's time to begin living your best moments, not just dreaming about them. They won't happen unless you take action.

The late author and teacher, Og Mandino, put it very succinctly, when he wrote, "action is the food and drink that nourishes success." The most detailed roadmap, the most intricate plan, even the most vivid dream is worth little unless you take steps to make it happen.

DEALING WITH ACTION-STOPPERS

If you are with me so far, then you are ready to take the plunge. The first thing you will have to deal with when you want to take action is your inertia. Generally speaking, a body at rest seeks to remain at rest. You tend to be comfortable with familiar things. So, even if your current situation is not ideal, it's at least familiar. And that appeals to you more than the unknown that lurks beyond your comfort zone.

Charlie is a 48-year-old father of two, who nearly died three years ago from a heart attack. Three of his four coronary arteries were blocked and open-heart surgery literally saved his life. Following the procedure, his heart was "as good as new," but his doctors told him that, if he did not change his diet and get more exercise, it would not be long before it deteriorated back to its deadly pre-surgical condition.

For about six months, Charlie did well. He exercised regularly, lost weight, and stayed away from his beloved fast foods. It appeared his near-death experience had made a new man of him. Then things began to revert.

He found that his exercise regimen was interfering with other important things in his life, so he stopped going to the gym and did calisthenics at home. This gave him more time to get back to some of his more familiar habits, such as watching TV, accompanied by snacking. Soon he was allowing himself the occasional trip to McDonalds. Then the occasional visit became more frequent. At some point in all of this the calisthenics stopped.

I'll spare you the details. Suffice it to say that it has been just about three years since his heart attack, and Charlie has gained all his weight back. He has begun having chest pain again and his doctors say that two of the three grafts on his heart have become blocked.

You'd think such a close brush with death would inspire a guy to do something different, especially with those two kids of his who are counting on him. It would appear that those incentives were no match for the lure of the familiar in Charlie's life.

Here's the startling news. Charlie is not an isolated example. In fact Charlie represents the overwhelming majority of those who go through this experience. Listen to what Dr. Edward Miller, Dean of the medical school and CEO of the hospital at Johns Hopkins University, has to say about the nearly 2 million people per year who undergo the same type of cardiac surgery as Charlie. "If you look at people after coronary artery bypass grafting two years later, 90% of them have not changed their lifestyles."

Apparently there are some things worse than death and one of them is living without the familiar taste of fatty fast food.

Face it. Whether you're up to your eyeballs in Big Macs or just way too comfortable on your "couchmaster," it's probably going to take a concerted burst of energy and resolve to get you started. Then, once you have overcome your inertia, if you are like most of us, you will next encounter an even bigger obstacle: fear.

What is your fear when it comes to taking humor action? Everybody has one, though some are more formidable than others. When I conducted a survey, the obstacle to effective humor action most often reported to me was fear of failure *(they won't think I'm funny)*. Others high on the list included fear of losing control *(people will get carried away or abuse the situation)*, fear of rejection *(they'll lose respect for me)*, inexperience *(I'll fall flat on my face)*, denial of the need for change *(I'm having enough fun already)*, fear of the enormity of the task *(I could never get them all laughing)* and fear of inadequate information *(I might unknowingly offend someone)*. All of these fears can stop your humor actions in their tracks if you let them.

This should neither surprise you, nor disable you. Inaction is a fear-based strategy, because it involves moving away from an undesirable outcome. You have discovered in this book that you are fully equipped to face down your fear. You have learned that there is no better antidote for fear than fun. Humor action is a fun-based decision, because, when you act, you are moving toward a positive goal.

If you have practiced the first five steps in this book, you are ready to take on whatever fear may arise at this point. Review the smile strategies you just learned and notice how nearly all of them address one or more of the fears I've just named.

Take, for example, the most common fear, that of failure. What is failure to you? I can assure you that the only real failure is that of not starting. If you "start with heart" and follow the dictates of your humor nature, you simply can't fail. You are assured of getting what you need and that is the truest measure of success. The smile strategies—**Welcome Your Mistakes**, **Expect The Unexpected**, **Honor Your Defeats** and **Celebrate Everything**, among others—will help you put this fear to flight.

Thomas Edison is recognized as one of the greatest inventors of all time. Before he was through, he held thousands of patents. However, for each patent he acquired there were scores of ideas that didn't work out.

Once he was asked if the high failure rate discouraged him. His answer was that he never considered a "failed" prototype a true failure, since it eliminated one model that didn't work, thus bringing him one step closer to the one that would.

What about the fear of losing control? It's true that once you take a humor action you have no control of the consequences. People might get carried away. The key to undermining this fear is to recognize that you have misled yourself if you think that holding back action gives you control. Consequences will occur with or without your action, and in neither case will you be calling the shots. If you are willing to settle for positively influencing the outcome instead of controlling it, your chances will be better if you act rather than if you hold back. Smile strategies such as **Let Go Frequently**, **Turn It Over**, **Take Charge of What You Can**, **Enjoy The Game**, and **Accept the Things You Cannot Change** ought to be useful here.

A youthful CEO was sharing her reflections on her award-winning success.

"I think the most important distinction I was able to make early on is the difference between controlling people and leading them. People want to be led, but they resent being controlled.

"I want to be a leader who expands the options and opportunities of my people. You can't do that by controlling them. So, I've learned to just set the direction, and then let people loose to create the progress.

"They'll think of things I would have overlooked. In the end they'll create a product that exceeds my imagination, but I'll get credit for leading them to it. That's a good deal for me, and all it takes is giving up a little control at the outset."

Southwest Airlines founder and first CEO Herb Kelleher once wrote, "I've never had control and I never wanted it. If you create an environment where people truly participate, you don't need control. They know what needs to be done and they do it."

If it's the fear of rejection that paralyzes you, smile strategies will be a solution for you as well. **Believe In Yourself**, **Laugh With Yourself**, **Admit When You Are Wrong** and **Choose Progress Over Perfection** are specific strategies I would recommend, although you may discover others that you prefer (such as **Give Whatever You Want to Receive**).

The effect that you are seeking is the realization that when people reject you, it is actually nothing personal.

Audrey, a recent graduate of drama school was trying to establish herself as a professional actress. Four hopeful auditions had resulted in four painful rejections and she found herself very discouraged.

Breaking down in her agent's office over the most recent rejection, she confessed her heartbreak and announced her intention to quit and go home to a more secure life.

Her agent happened to know one of the producers of the show that had just rejected Audrey and he placed a call to him immediately. The producer explained that everyone had been favorably impressed with her audition, but the director needed a natural blonde for a swimming pool scene in which a wig would be out of the question. Audrey was a brunette.

After sharing this information with her, Audrey's agent told her, "You have no idea what any director is looking for and no control over 95% of the reasons for your rejection. You must learn to see it for what it is—a rejection of a part, not a rejection of you."

Audrey summarized what she learned from that experience. "I decided then and there to make every audition nothing more than a chance to meet people, my chief goal being to make contact with the director and allow him to see my face. Beyond that, all I'm doing is practicing for the day that I'm right for the part. Once I've done the best I can do, I don't take it personally if I don't fit the role."

You can learn from Audrey because, in a sense, everyone you meet is a director looking to cast you in a preconceived role. You may not fit the part the director thinks she needs you to play and, frankly, if you knew what she had in mind, you might not want to. In any case the last thing you want to do is take it as a rejection of the best you have to give. This is especially true when your actions are inspired by your humor nature.

When someone rejects your humor action it clearly has more

to do with them than with you. Perhaps they have just weathered a painful personal setback and, for the moment, just can't laugh. Or maybe they are intimidated by the audacity of your action. It might be that they are just not in the mood for fun. Big deal! You should not infer any disrespect for you on their part. If anything, they probably respect you more for your courage to reach out.

How could their rejection be personal? These people don't know you at all. It is far more likely to be nothing more than an emotional defensiveness or an unwillingness to make an effort to understand you (in a word, laziness). Why would you want these people in your support system anyway? They have nothing to contribute. The last thing you would want is to think like they do. Let your smile strategies assist you in celebrating the lifting of their collective "dead weight" from your worthy shoulders.

My patient, Candace, has maintained her optimal weight for almost two years. Understand, however, that during the preceding decade, Candace was anywhere from 60 to 130 pounds overweight. She sought my help when she became suicidal because of her weight problem.

After struggling for over ten years, how did Candace finally lose the weight? And, more important, how did she keep it off?

Candace always knew what her desired weight was and had always worked toward that goal. Her biggest obstacle, however, was not the frozen dessert aisle at her super market.

Candace's mother had rejected her because of her weight problem, telling her repeatedly, "Nobody loves a fat person." Candace had internalized those words and felt unworthy of acceptance every time she fell short of her mother's exacting standards.

Talk about a recipe for failure. Candace had only one condition under which she was willing to accept herself: perfection.

Once Candace was able to appreciate that progress was an

event worth celebrating, she began to regard every positive step for what it was—a step in the right direction. She began to accept herself as "a work in progress" worthy of love at every step of her journey. When her attitude became more accepting of herself, it wasn't long before her mother began to follow suit.

Inexperience is frequently reported as an obstruction to humor action. "How can I hope to succeed? I'm no good at telling jokes. I don't have any experience or credentials." Sound familiar? If this is one of your personal impasses, stop and consider this. Success and health both require growth; growth involves movement from familiar (safe) territory to unfamiliar ground. It figures then, that, if your action is going to provide you with healthy growth, it's going to take you into unfamiliar territory. In that case, of course you are going to lack experience. You've never walked that path before. But, you will learn by taking the humor action. That's the whole point of growth.

Roger was the first amongst our group of friends to turn sixty years old. At his birthday celebration, I asked him, "Roger, what's it like to be sixty?"

He shot back, "I don't know. I've never been this age before."

The smile strategies you will find especially helpful when inexperience is your obstruction include **Listen Very Carefully**, **Expect the Unexpected**, **Be Constantly Curious** and **Ask the Dumb Question**.

Next, let's look at the denial of the need for action. If this often paralyzes you, believe me, you have lots of company. By convincing yourself that there is no immediate need for humor action, you can justify saying or doing nothing. However, I must warn you that it may be too late for you to use this excuse. At least I hope so. If you want to justify staying on the sidelines by using this rationale, you will have to toss aside nearly everything you have learned in the first five steps of this book.

The smile strategy **Tell the Truth** is practically foolproof in addressing this obstruction. If you are willing to tell it like it is, you won't be able to maintain your denial of the need for action for very long. We are all really hungry for more fun.

My personal "favorite" in this list of action-stoppers is the fear of the enormity of the task. I can immobilize myself immediately by telling myself that the task is too grand for me to ever complete. In the case of humor action, this fear takes the form of "stage fright." I foresee myself "running out of gas" long before the journey is complete (before I've won them over to fun).

When I'm up against these thoughts inside my head, here's what I've learned to do. I remind myself that no significant accomplishment can ever be rendered by one single act, no matter how energetic or dramatic it might be. It always takes a series of actions.

It is said that an admirer once asked the famous sculptor Rodin, "How are you able to transform such a huge piece of rock into the likeness of a beautiful human body?"

Reportedly, the master's profound answer was, "It's not as complicated as you might think. All I do is chip away everything that does not look like a beautiful human body."

Author James Collins, in his book, *Good To Great*, writes about the "flywheel concept," which he considers to be a chief characteristic of the forward movement of any great company. It holds that no significant breakthrough occurs as a result of one large move, but is instead the result of many smaller moves made repeatedly over an extended period of time. The series of "tiny" applications of energy move the wheel a little at a time, allowing its momentum to gradually become a greater and greater part of the total energy "package," until the "breakthrough" moment when momentum takes over and the motion becomes self-sustaining. It's like rocking a car back and forth when it is stuck in a snowdrift. One concerted effort has less chance of freeing the car than a succession of brief ones.

Once I remember this concept, then I can use the help of the smile strategy **Locate Your Target**. This teaches me to establish a series of short and medium term goals to fill in the gap between my inertia and the out of reach completion of my task. I can take the humor action, even if it doesn't get a thunderous "ovation."

Last but not least among our common action inhibitors is the fear of inadequate information. You can't act, or won't, because you don't have sufficient data to justify or support your action. What if someone is offended by your humor action, because of something you did not know about her? Of all the reasons that make us pause before acting, this one makes the most sense. If you don't have enough information, I think you should forestall taking action, but only long enough to fix it by taking another action first, namely getting the information you need. Use your common sense in assessing the mood and disposition of those around you. Ask pertinent questions. Then, get on with it.

Crossing a busy street is a great example. It would be foolish to forge ahead without pausing long enough to look both ways. However, once you establish that the coast is clear, it is equally foolish to dawdle before crossing. If it's a busy street, it won't remain clear for long.

On the off-chance that you "misjudge" a situation or person and, despite your best intentions, wind up offending with your humor action, it's quite sufficient to sincerely apologize, with reassurances that you had no intention to be hurtful. You may have to walk away respectfully, but don't give up on the humor action. There will be a better time and place. Nobody's perfect!

BROADENING YOUR RANGE OF ACTION

Once you have overcome your fears of taking action, you will want to sidestep one more trap that awaits you. It is the trap of too narrowly defining your action options. You might assume that unless you are charging forward into the fray, with guns blazing, producing raucous laughter, you are settling for something less than a fully effective humor action plan. In spite of all I've said about the need to be bold, effective humor action can take various forms. Sometimes, charging full-steam ahead is unwise. So here are a few additional things you might want to think about.

1. Inaction is a form of action

The parable of the talents in the Bible's New Testament (Matthew, Chapter 25) teaches that passivity is not the same thing as standing still. The servants who took action with the resources they were given were richly rewarded, whereas the one, who passively hoarded his talent, had it taken away and given to the others. Inaction in this case turned out to be a not-so-subtle form of moving backwards.

Nevertheless, there are situations in which taking no immediate action is the best action. You've heard of a strategic retreat. The important word here is strategic. Your strategic objective is to create a more positive environment. It is one thing to withhold action in order to move closer to your goals. Inactivity by default or immobilization by fear is quite another.

Since "true" inaction is not an option, the only choice is what action you will take.

We were gathered in the boardroom of a local corporation. I had been hired to consult with their human resources team in the development of a plan to raise morale in the workplace. After several meetings with their team, this was to be the much anticipated unveiling of the plan to the company's leaders.

The Vice President for Human Resources opened the meeting.

"Mr. Clark said he might be running a little late," he announced, referring to the CEO. "He asked us to start without him."

He proceeded to report on the 12-month plan that had been produced by the task force. It looked to me like the ideas were being received with enthusiasm, as heads nodded in agreement around the table.

Ten minutes into the presentation, the door opened slowly and Mr. Clark quietly entered the room.

"Don't mind me," he said. "Please continue as if I wasn't here."

A "strategic retreat" would have been a better option for Mr. Clark. Had he remained silent, the chances are that the positive momentum of the meeting could have been sustained, in spite of his late arrival. By speaking out, he made it impossible to follow his instructions. The tone of the meeting changed immediately. Heads stopped nodding. The presentation became more formal.

Try as he might, once he spoke up, there was no way the boss could be a "neutral" observer.

This leads us to a second thought about action.

2. Action is always an interaction

It is clear that all action is really interaction. There are no unilateral moves in life. Every action is a form of a reciprocal relationship. That means that everything you say or do has an impact on you as well as everyone else in your life. You saw evidence of this in the parable of the talents. Passivity is not what you may think. Like it or not, you are in the mix, one way or the other.

One of the most startling discoveries in all of science occurred in the latter part of the 20th century. For ages the scientific method had rested on the basic assumption that a passive and objective observer could witness a physical phenomenon without affecting the process in the least. Modern physics has put that erroneous assumption to rest by demonstrating that it is impossible to observe a process without affecting its outcome in some way. Complete passivity is out of the question.

I have experienced this reality in my clinical work with patients. My training in psychotherapy was from the Freudian model, which stresses that the therapist should strive to be totally passive, so as not to "contaminate" the patients' freedom to speak unilaterally and spontaneously during a session.

I realized how impossible this goal of "anonymity" was for me, when on the day following my learning of my college roommate's death, my patient opened the session by asking what had happened. Despite my best effort to keep it outside the session, she had come to know me too well not to sense that I was grieving. I have since learned that the therapeutic "blank screen" is about as transparent as the emperor's new clothes.

"When I'm at work I only talk to people who are already smiling," volunteered Betsy, a secretary working in a university research center. "When you ask somebody who's not smiling how they are doing, you usually get a complaint or something negative. Either that or they're too preoccupied. I feel like I'm interrupting something of dire importance. It brings me down. I don't need that. I take a smile as a signal that something positive can be transacted."

She continued, "Then one day it dawned on me that perhaps others felt the same way when approaching me. So, I tried to smile more. Guess what? Since I started that, I find more people smiling at me. Life is like a big mirror. The number of smiling people I see is a reflection of how much I'm smiling."

3. Words are a form of action

"Sticks and stones will break my bones, but words will never hurt me." We all remember that little childhood taunt. Turns out it's not true. Words are a powerful form of action that can have a very strong effect on both the speaker and the listener.

Here's another one you can throw away: "Talk is cheap." Yes, it's a lot easier to talk about most things than to actually do them, but you can at times pay a high price for the idle words you utter.

Jim, a recovering cancer patient, showed up for his support group one afternoon sporting purple hair. Everyone feared that he perhaps had fallen prey to a weird and belated "side effect" from his chemotherapy. He was quick to reassure us.

"It's kind of embarrassing, but it's nothing serious," he announced. "I simply lost a bet."

He explained that he had made a deal with his 15-year-old daughter. Both claiming to be the best "Scrabble" players in the family, they challenged one another to a "winner take all" match up. She had agreed that if he won, she would give up her "punk" look and get a "normal" haircut. In return, if she was able to beat him, he agreed to dye his hair whatever color she chose.

Guess who won.

"She told me I didn't really have to go through with it, but fair is fair," he chuckled. "I certainly would have held her to the deal, if I had won."

"Anyway," he added, "it'll all grow out in a few weeks."

As life goes on, the intention to be "as good as one's word" is a valuable asset to success. Dependability, reliability and integrity open doors of opportunity and elicit cooperation from others. Your words have great potential power. Choose them wisely.

Whenever you speak a word out loud, it plants a seed in your own mind and in the minds of all who hear you. Your word is your unique creative tool. You can use it against yourself or on your behalf.

Brenda "condemns" herself with her own words whenever she attempts to tell a joke. She always leads up to the joke by apologizing, "I can never tell jokes, but maybe you can get the gist of this one, even if I mess up the punch line."

Well, of course nobody laughs at her jokes. Her words predict failure and create that expectation in everyone's minds, including her own—a self-fulfilling prophecy.

Be careful not to speak against yourself. Others will believe what you say and so will you. You don't want to poison the well before you drink the water.

Now that you have looked at your fear(s) and thought through some action options, I sense you are primed for action, revving your engines and raring to go. There is, however one last potential stumbling block to be eliminated, and I think it's best to do it now.

4. Dispensing With Feelings of Guilt

Because you are perfectly imperfect, we both know that, when you take action, you will at times make mistakes. You will sometimes choose the wrong words and, of course, once they've been spoken, you can't take them back. At other times you may act in such a way as to cause unintended pain, or simply make matters worse, despite your best intentions. You may even have cause to regret your actions.

In short, if you act responsibly, you will sometimes be responsible for a wrong action. It is not easy to recognize and accept responsibility when your actions have an undesirable effect. It helps if you recognize the difference between being guilty and feeling guilt.

This may sound like a strange sentiment coming from a psychiatrist, but I think the concept of guilt is, for the most part, bogus. If you were to tell me you *were guilty*, I would take it to mean that you had deliberately or accidentally done something wrong, and were now recognizing the error of your ways. That would make sense. If you had indeed done something wrong, then by definition you would be guilty of the wrongdoing. My advice to you would be to make restitution, as best you could, and, while paying your debt, learn all you could from your mistake. Then leave your mistake where it belongs—in the past—and concentrate on present realities.

If, on the other hand, you were to tell me you were *feeling guilt*, I would see you as taking yourself way too seriously. I would take it to mean that you were attempting to prop up your over-sized ego by taking responsibility for something you had no control over, and thus, by your suffering, prove that you really have that much power, and should have exercised it. That would make no sense at all. In which case, my advice would be, "Get over yourself!"

Guilty is a verdict. Guilt is an ego trip. Guilt enables you to remain self-centered, while appearing to be focused on others. Guilt is really all about you, not the others who may have been affected by your wrongdoing.

Your humor nature respects a guilty verdict, but will have no truck with a guilt-inflated ego. It recognizes guilt as a fear-based overly serious manipulation, inspired by an egotistical refusal to accept realistic limitations. It will do everything it can to puncture that pompous stance. If you want your humor nature working for you, you must let go of guilt. It is a malignant form of seriousness that will hold you back and impair your health.

Patricia came to me for help during her third year of medical school. Unable to sleep at night, she was having problems with constant fatigue.

Although she was doing well in school, Patricia's fatigue had begun to affect her performance by causing her to fall asleep in class and during clinical procedures. She was afraid that her frequent "catnaps" were getting worse and, in time, would get her in trouble with her instructors and colleagues.

As she talked about her medical training, it was clear that Patricia had drawn great satisfaction from "getting through" the first two years, which were filled with hours of pressure-packed reading and studying. Her current difficulties didn't arise until she began her third year clinical assignments, in which she was expected to learn at the patients' bedsides rather than from the book.

She admitted that she wasn't enjoying patient contact as much as she thought she would. She felt overwhelmed by the intimacy and the responsibility. This led me to ask about how she had decided on medicine as a career.

"I owe it to my family and to myself to become a doctor," was her reply. "My older brother, George, was killed by a drunken driver when I was a sophomore in high school, He was in his third year of college, home for the holidays, and was coming to pick me up at the movies the night the accident happened. I know it's crazy, but I have always felt guilt over his death. He'd still be alive today, if I hadn't asked him to pick me up that night."

"The accident devastated all of us," she continued. "George had been planning to be a doctor for as long as I can remember. So, I decided that I would go to medical school in his place. I want to become the doctor the world has been deprived of because of me. Nobody put any pressure on me. It was my own idea."

I asked Patricia what she would be doing with her life if she weren't trying to work out her guilt this way. It took some urging to get an answer.

Reluctantly she shared with me that she wanted to be a painter. She had always wanted to be an artist of some kind.

Over months of intensive, sometimes agonizing, dialogue, Patricia came to realize that she really wasn't comfortable in medicine and, more to the point, her guilt over his brother's death was a disguised wish to be powerful enough to bring George "back to life" by being the doctor he would have been. Once she was able to let go of those unrealistic expectations, she could truly grieve the loss of her brother.

Only then could Patricia recognize that the very best way to honor her brother and her parents would be to "honor" herself by pursuing a career that would allow her to develop her own unique gifts as a person and an artist.

Today, she has a successful career in graphic design and is highly respected as a teacher and mentor of young artists.

So, the challenge is to be guilty of your mistakes and learn from them without feeling guilt. Don't overreact. Sometimes it's necessary to learn first what not to do. If you keep in mind the quote you read from Thomas Edison, earlier in this chapter, about how valuable each "failed" prototype was in moving him closer to his eventual success, you'll find that even your mistakes will make a positive contribution to your progress.

5. Setting Things In Motion

OK. Now you are ready for the first tangible test of your commitment to your humor nature. Are you willing to act on the inspiration and energy it offers you? Will you allow joy to be the highest priority in your life? Making fun your first priority is the single biggest step you can take toward your ultimate happiness and success.

Why is this true? It is because, as you now can see, happiness is not a byproduct of any activity or achievement. There is nothing in this world that can make you happy. In fact, some of the happiest people I've ever met have nothing and achieve less. A group of Buddhist monks I encountered were ecstatically happy. Yet they had forsworn the ownership and collection of the same material possessions that you and I have often looked to for happiness. While you would never associate happiness with a deadly terminal disease, I have met scores of kids diagnosed with muscular dystrophy who have adopted the indomitable spirit of fun espoused by their hero, Jerry Lewis. They are happier than you could ever imagine.

What have these people done to achieve unpredictable levels of happiness that have eluded some of the world's "richest" individuals? Precisely the same thing I'm encouraging you to do right now. By practicing actions that focus their attention on the immediate experience of joy in the moment, they put fun first. They have their fun wherever they find it, just as you did way back at the beginning of your life. They have not surrendered their goals or aspirations. They have merely made fun the foundation of all their activities.

Of course you know by now that the word "fun" may have a different meaning for every person. This book will never dictate what should be fun for you. However, some generalizations apply. The common "denominators" of fun are: enjoying yourself, not harming anyone (including yourself), celebrating your imperfect perfection and motivating your mind body and spirit. In other words, you're having fun whenever you are doing something fulfilling, engaging and uplifting.

When you were a youngster riding in the back seat of your family's car, your most frequent question was, "Are we there yet?" In many ways you are still asking that question about your goals and aspirations for health and happiness: "Am I there yet?"

I want you to stop asking that question. It is, and always was, the wrong question. You are "there" already. You have everything you need for happiness. The question that will set it in motion is, "Am I having fun yet?" That is the critical question.

If the answer to "Am I having fun?" is "No," you must change that situation before you do anything else. Fortunately, with this book as your resource, your ability to make any activity fun is now a reality. Why should you wait any longer to be happier? Start having fun first right now and watch what happens.

I know. I'm advocating a selfish move. We've discussed this before. Health is selfish. Healing is selfish. Success is selfish. Don't confuse selfish with self-centered. The universe doesn't revolve around you, but you are by far the most important person in your life. You can't experience your best unless you take the initiative for yourself. I can't do it for you—no one can.

And, don't hand me that altruism argument. You're not much good for others if you aren't at your best.

So, be proactive on your own behalf and do something now. Let me repeat the assignment. It is simply to have fun before you do anything else. You're worth the effort.

Alma is a 72-year-old woman who, since her husband died of cancer fifteen years ago, has been volunteering daily as a receptionist at a local cancer center. Everyone who passes through the doors of that center finds Alma's energy and enthusiasm remarkable. Despite all the fearful and sad things she witnesses, as people struggle desperately to survive their cancers, she never seems to have a bad day. Her good cheer and optimism are constantly at a high level.

One day I commended her on her seemingly boundless supply of good will and positive thoughts, and I asked her how she did it.

She winked at me and said, "I schedule my vacations first."

"How does that help?" I wondered.

"Probably not the way you think," she responded. "I love to travel. So, that's the first thing I plan every year. And I tell the clinic manager every January which weeks I'll be gone for the whole year. She knows that, no matter what else is going on in the clinic for those weeks, my time off is not negotiable."

"So by looking forward to your upcoming trips, you can maintain your rosy disposition through thick and thin," I commented.

"Not exactly," she cautioned me. "My trips aren't my compensation for working in this environment. The work I do doesn't make me need a reward. It's the other way around. The trips make me want to do this work. I come here to give back the joy I get from traveling."

Alma's distinction is subtle, but critical. It underlines the concept of being proactive and it will enable you to unleash the full power of your healthy humor nature. If you schedule fun activities only to reward or compensate yourself for hard work, or to provide an incentive for working harder, you will be missing the point. Fun is the fuel that makes the hard work possible and, as such, you are wise to fill your tank in advance.

Our friend Jenny is a strict advocate of Garfield's policy, "Eat dessert first." Whenever she attends a buffet, she invariably goes to the dessert table first and brings her dessert selection to her place. Then she goes back for the rest of the meal.

"You never know how long those dessert selections are going to be there," she explains. "Sometimes the best desserts disappear fast, while I've never seen them run out of mashed potatoes and green beans. There's plenty of time for those items. Besides, when I know which dessert I'm going to have, it inspires me to make good choices for my entrée and I don't overeat."

I wonder if that's what Garfield has been trying to tell us all along.

Jenny's rationale is difficult to criticize.

If you are unwilling to take prompt action and to be proactive on your own behalf you still have plenty of company. You are exhibiting a behavior that is shared by unsuccessful and unhealthy people the world over. It's called procrastination. Oh, we call it many things in an effort to rationalize this nonproductive hesitancy. We even go so far as to suggest that postponing immediate pleasure in the service of a "higher" goal is often a desirable sign of personal maturity and stability.

That's usually said with an apparent disdain for childlikeness, because you will never see children postponing their fun. Children just do not procrastinate when it comes to enjoying themselves. They are comfortable and unapologetic about their spontaneity. That observation alone should be enough to set off warning alarms when, as adults, we catch ourselves procrastinating.

Paradoxically, procrastination is the one thing you should put off, if you want to be happier right now.

So, as they say in the Nike ads, "Just Do It!" **Do something fun for yourself at once.** Remember it can be something as simple as a smile or a kind word offered to the next person you meet, not because they need it (of course they *do*), but because you deserve the benefits of taking action now.

Step Seven: Improve With Improv

The house lights go down and as the audience quiets itself, a lone actor walks out to center stage.

"May I have a suggestion of an occupation?" he requests.

There follows a cacophony of shouts from the audience, out of which the actor picks "plastic surgeon."

"Thank you," he says, as he steps back from the edge of the stage.

An actress emerges from stage left and walks to the foot lights.

"May I have another suggestion of an occupation?" she asks.

Again, a torrent of words is heard, out of which the actress hears "rodeo clown."

As the actress thanks the audience and joins her colleague, a third actor arrives from stage right and addresses the audience.

"Now we need a setting," he announces. More shouts from the audience seem to coalesce around "a Caribbean cruise ship!"

"And an event," adds the actor.

"A first date!"

"OK!" the third actor summarizes, "We have a plastic surgeon and a rodeo clown together on a cruise ship. The occasion is their first date. Proceed."

And with that, the first two actors launch into a portrayal of their assigned roles, creating a spirited and engaging dialogue around the occasion of this most unusual "first date" and their vocational differences. Soon other actors join them—the captain of the ship, a cocktail waitress, other couples along for the cruise—and a coherent scene develops out of four random audience suggestions.

Sitting in the audience, we witness an amazing display of teamwork and mutual support. There is creativity, flexibility, high energy and, above all, laughter. The actors themselves seem surprised at some of the scene's spontaneous twists and turns.

The fun spills over the footlights. As "authors" of the characters and premise, the audience enjoys a certain pride of creative ownership as they watch the actors succeed on stage.

This scene is familiar to anyone who has attended a performance of improvisation theatre. Spontaneity, high energy, creativity, enthusiasm, mutual support, resilience and teamwork are standard fare in improv, but fun and laughter are the key ingredients—so much so that for most of us, the word "improv" has become practically synonymous with comedy.

Improv not only creates a wonderful night at the theater, it also serves as a model for achieving the health and happiness we crave, a model made to order for your humor nature.

Think about it. Wouldn't you want those same high levels of energy, creativity, enthusiasm, support, spontaneity, resilience, teamwork, and fun in your life and work? Wouldn't a work environment with all those characteristics, plus an involved audience (customers), have an excellent chance of success? And, if you were the main "actor" in your life, wouldn't you want your "audience" to have a vested interest in your success?

Beyond these powerful ingredients, there is another reason why I recommend the improv model to you: It is a true reflection of reality. When you get right down to it, isn't life really one huge improvisation? Does anyone have the script? Let's face it. With nothing more than a few guiding principles to light the way, we are all pretty much making it up as we go along, and hoping for the best. You really don't know what's around the next corner or over the next hill.

Therefore, it stands to reason that the better you can be at improvisation, the happier and more successful you're going to become. Step Seven challenges you to learn the secrets of successful improv, so that its powerful benefits are available to you every day of your life.

You will become a more successful improviser by studying how the professionals do it onstage. Granted, some people will be better at it than others, but the fact remains that each of us can improve our improv skills, if we are willing to learn and practice.

Professional improvisers agree that there are certain basic rules of improv that must be adopted and followed. I have identified six I want to teach you. I think you will find them invigorating to your humor nature, even if you never plan to perform on stage. The rules of improv are:

—*Accept Every Premise*

—*Always Say, "Yes, AND..."*

—*Expand and Elevate Every Idea*

—*Act It Out*

—*Do Your Best*

—*Celebrate All Progress*

1. ACCEPT EVERY PREMISE

To succeed as an improviser, you must have an open mind. If you are resistant to suggestions you will quickly become a liability to yourself and the others on your team. Unconditional acceptance is your goal here. Remember that acceptance is not the same thing as approval or endorsement. You may not agree with the choice that is offered you, but to have any success at all you must accept it.

If you and I are beginning a scene together, and you say to me, "That's an interesting hat you're wearing," I am obliged to accept your suggestion. If I refuse by answering, "I'm not wearing a hat," the scene is over before it has had a chance to breathe, and, as the scene-killer, I'm probably not going to be invited back for more improv.

If I want to succeed, I must accept that, if you say I have a hat on my head, by golly, I've got a hat on until I find a way to take it off. Once I accept that premise, I am free to go anywhere I want with it. I may choose to say, "Thanks for noticing the hat. It belonged to my great, great grandfather, who wore it in the civil war." Or. I could say, "Please forgive my bad manners. I meant to take my hat off when I came in here." Note how either answer keeps the possibilities open for the further development of our scene.

Accepting the premise is really all about accepting possibilities that might not be clear to you at the moment. This rule encourages compliance, and compliance is enhanced when you keep an open mind. Preconceived notions of what ought to be will get in the way of your improvisation skills. Notice how smile strategies like **Expect the Unexpected** and **Challenge All Assumptions** will help you keep your mind open to unimagined possibilities. Unconditional acceptance may not guarantee your success, but it is a necessary first step toward increasing your chances.

Everyday Application

Let's suppose, when you go in for your annual physical this year, your doctor tells you she detects an abnormality in your blood sugar level, a possible early sign of Type II Adult Onset Diabetes. This unwelcome news surprises you because you have experienced no symptoms of diabetes and you feel fine. You're tempted to doubt the significance of this "abnormality," by chalking it up to a laboratory error, but your doctor suggests following it up with more testing, a reasonable recommendation under the circumstances.

At that moment you have the same choices as any improviser. You can reject or accept the possibility that you have early diabetes. If you reject this possibility, you will probably refuse the additional tests your doctor is suggesting. If you choose to accept the possibility, you're likely to go along with reasonable efforts to learn more about your condition.

Keep in mind, the key issue is whether or not you accept the possibility of your having diabetes. For the moment, your doctor's advice is not the issue. If her recommendations strike you as an "overreaction," you can always seek a second opinion. But, by keeping an open mind about the possibility of the diagnosis, you are giving yourself more chances to be successful, if it turns out to be true.

If you do happen to have early diabetes, and you close your mind to it, you have already decreased your chances of successfully managing the illness. By rejecting the possibility, you will be giving the disease more time to gain a foothold undetected. Only by accepting the news at the earliest possible moment, no matter how unsavory it is to you, can you hope to maximize your chances of a successful response.

In this same way, **Accepting Every Premise** will make you more successful in every aspect of your life.

Improv Exercise

There is a common improv game that will help you practice this rule of acceptance. I call it "The Alphabetical Conversation." Recruit a friend or colleague to play it with you. It goes like this:

Agree with your partner to have a conversation about "nothing in particular." In fact, the conversation doesn't even have to make sense. It's just for fun. The only rule you both must follow is that each comment must start in alphabetical order. By that I mean that the first person to speak begins his/her statement with a word that begins with "A." The other person then responds, but must start his/her comment with a word that begins with "B." Then, person #1 speaks again with a comment that begins with "C." Back and forth it goes until you have gone through the entire alphabet in order. Remember the conversation can be completely nonsensical, but it must conform to the alphabetical rule.

For example, you might start by saying to me, "Are you interested in this game?"

And, I might answer, "Bantering back and forth can be fun."

To which you might respond, "Can you believe how silly we must sound?"

Then, me: "Don't you think it's fun?"

You: "Especially when there's nothing to lose."

Me: "Fine!"

You: "Great!"

Me: "Heck, this is getting easier by the second."

And on and on, until we get to "Z": "Zounds, we made it through the alphabet."

Of course to play this game successfully, you must accept the silly premise of the alphabetical rule. Once you do, as long as you are willing to surrender to your humor nature, you'll have fun and stimulate your imagination.

The game need not be confined to only two players. I have used it as a warm up exercise before important meetings of our clinic staff. We just go around the table, each in turn advancing one more letter until we complete the alphabet. Sometimes we will even go through the alphabet twice. We have found it's a great way to open our minds for creative thought and "get the juices flowing."

The success and fun you can have, once you learn to "accept every premise," proves the old adage: "You've got to go along to get along."

2. ALWAYS SAY, "YES, AND..."

At first glance, this rule doesn't look like much, but, if you're like most of us, it will dramatically change the way you respond to others. Right now, when someone brings a new idea to your attention you are much more likely to respond with "Yes, BUT..." than "Yes, AND..."

Why? Because, saying "Yes, BUT" is a way to slow things down and keep control. It amounts to giving your support and taking it back, all in the same sentence. Instead of embracing the new idea, "Yes, BUT" allows you to keep it at arm's length. It's a way to play it safe—if something goes wrong, it's not your fault. At times it can even represent resistance.

The point is, we are all in the habit of saying "Yes, BUT" to everything. Remember, we have already acknowledged we are creatures of habit, with a strong aversion to the unfamiliar. If nothing else, "Yes, BUT..." robs you and those around you of precious energy.

Everyday Application

Let's suppose you are in a planning meeting at work. Someone enthusiastically makes a proposal for an event that will both improve the company's public relations and benefit the local community. As the financial officer, you like the idea, but it's your responsibility to report that there is no room for it in this year's budget. So you say, "*Yes*, that's a great idea, Ted, *but* we have no money for it in the budget."

What happens to the idea? You can almost hear the brakes squealing as it comes to a screeching halt. What happens to Ted's enthusiasm? How likely is it that Ted will want to present his next great idea *("Shot down again!")*?

Now imagine changing just one word in your response. It's still the same proposal and still the same "empty" budget, but this time, as the financial officer, you say, "*Yes*, that's a great idea, Ted, *and* we'll have to be creative to find the funding for it." You have still told him that the money's not there, but look at the difference that one word makes.

Not only is Ted's idea and enthusiasm still alive and well, but you have increased the momentum by encouraging "creativity" in the funding. You have added support for the fledgling idea. Others are more likely to jump on board with suggestions. Your use of the word "and" has kept options open, whereas "but" had closed them down.

Success in improv is about keeping options open; success in life is about the same thing. When you use "and" instead of "but" you are cooperating in a way that lends some of your energy to the effort, increasing the likelihood of synergy with your "teammates," and thereby, your ultimate success.

Improv Exercises

I have used an exercise that I call "Yes, AND, Down the Lane" as a warm up exercise for any group. It's also a good way to discover how automatic your "Yes, BUTs" have become. It's easily done while sitting around a table.

One person begins by making a comment (about anything) to the person on her left. The second person responds by saying "Yes, AND," then turns to the person on his left and makes his comment. Each person in the circle does the same maneuver, listening to the comment of the person on her right, then repeating "Yes, and..," as she turns to make a comment to the person on her left. Quite often, despite the deliberate focus of the exercise, a "Yes, BUT" will slip out.

A common improv game that will help you practice saying, "Yes, AND…" is one I call "The Wizard." It makes a great party game. It requires a minimum of six people. Here's how it is played:

Three individuals are selected to be "the wizard." The object of the game is for the wizard to answer any question posed to it, no matter how perplexing the issue involved. All three individuals making up the wizard participate in each answer, one word at a time. That means that each gets to add one word, and one word only, before passing the answer-in-progress on to the next person. No one player controls the answer, because he/she can only input every third word. It's as though three equal brains were cohabiting one body. The answer goes on until there is consensus among the three that it is complete, or at least sufficient.

Those not selected to become the wizard make up the "audience." They will be asking the questions. They are encouraged to ask the questions that have always perplexed them, those questions for which they've never gotten satisfactory answers. "Why is the sky blue?" "What is the meaning of life?" "Where have all the flowers gone?" Stuff like that.

The answers produced by the one word at a time trio are sometimes remarkably profound, in ways that could not have been anticipated or planned. A recent example occurred during a workshop I held for insurance company executives. We happened to be taping the Wizard Game, and here is the transcription of one of the answers we got:

ME: "Wizard, we want to know. What is the true meaning of life?"
WIZARD: "Laugh ... love ... live ... enjoy ... because ... the ... true ... meaning ... of ... life ... is ... that ... it ... has ... no ... meaning."

There is no tolerance for "Yes, BUT" in the process of the wizard game. The players must simply accept what they are handed, add one word, then pass it on. It's a powerful illustration of the spirit of "Yes, AND..."

3. EXPAND AND ELEVATE EVERY IDEA

In improv theater, each performer makes it her responsibility to develop the existing premise to its highest level, whether or not it's the idea she would have selected. This is the rule that produces the remarkable teamwork we observe amongst the members of an improv troupe. Regardless of its origins, every idea gets its chance to shine as brilliantly as it can, and who scores the points and gets the credit is less important, than having the team win. There are no bad ideas. No one is hung out to dry. When teammates are "watching your back" like that, it becomes easier to take the risks that are necessary for success.

Besides teamwork, this improv rule also enhances the quality of your product or outcome, by discouraging the temptation to compromise standards just for a quick payoff. No "cheap laughs" here. Successful performers aim for the "high road," even if it takes a little longer. The parallels to everyday life are obvious, don't you think?

Expanding and elevating every idea is a great way to help others succeed. By now, I'm sure you've noticed that the best insurance for your own success is your willingness to be instrumental in the successes of those around you.

Everyday Practice

Let's return to the issue of your hypothetical diabetes problem we discussed earlier. Suppose, upon further investigation, you learn that you do indeed have diabetes. Now the challenge is to develop an effective treatment plan.

If you left it completely up to your doctor to call the shots at this point, you might be unwittingly limiting your success in developing an optimal plan, because no matter how brilliant she may be, your doctor doesn't have your unique perspective on your problem. This is where expanding and elevating every idea makes good practical sense for you. You can enhance still further your chances for success by taking the initiative to do your own "research" and learn as much as you can about diabetes. It's possible that you will "discover" something that your doctor is overlooking, and can bring it to her attention. Your informed questions can be a stimulus for your doctor's research on your behalf. In other words, by adding your "effort" to the thinking process, you become a collaborator with your physician, as together you and she lay out a more comprehensive array of resources. That's teamwork.

Improv Exercise

The Limerick Game is a standard performance piece for most improv troupes. It clearly illustrates the beauty of the "expand and elevate" rule. The game requires five "performers" and an "audience" of at least 4 or 5 people. It is one of the favorites at my workshops.

The object of the limerick game is to construct a limerick about any subject or topic that is suggested. A limerick, of course, is a poem consisting of five lines. The first two lines are longer and rhyme with each other. The third and fourth lines are shorter and also rhyme with each other (but, not with the first two). The fifth and final line is as long as the first two and rhymes with them as well:

A wonderful thing is your laughter
So, let it be heard from the rafters
With your beautiful smile
And your personal style
You'll accomplish whatever you're after.

There's an example of a limerick. It may be the "cleanest" one you've ever read. Therein lies a major challenge in playing this game. Most of the limericks you have heard throughout life have been bawdy and crass, heavily laden with sexual allusions and innuendos. Avoiding such references will require participants to truly *expand* and *elevate* their output. Hence if you ever play this game, I recommend you declare the word "Nantucket" off limits—for obvious reasons.

You start the game by selecting a "limerick team," consisting of five individuals (one for each line of the poem format). These team members line up shoulder to shoulder. The audience members then suggest a subject about which they want to hear a limerick. The first team member in line gives the opening line and each in turn is responsible for the next line of the poem, ending when the fifth member offers a line that rhymes with the first two.

Then, the team members rotate in the same fashion as a volleyball team, so that each has a different assignment for the next requested limerick. The requests can range to almost any topic or subject—holidays, seasons, professions, famous people, cities, sports—although it's best not to get into items of gender, nationality or race. By the third or fourth limerick the team members usually develop an *esprit de corps*, as they discover how to feed one another lines that are fun to rhyme. It is remarkable how quickly a strong spirit of unity arises.

4. ACT IT OUT

It's an old cliché that "actions speak louder than words," but it has never been truer than on the stage of improv theatre. Words have a great deal of power and influence, but when movement accompanies them, the impact is maximized. In fact, many of the most effective moments in improv contain no words at all—only actions.

Successful improvisers "dramatize" their ideas with facial expressions, tone of voice and bodily movements. That's the key.

They "act **it** out." What is the "it" that they are acting out? **It** is their vision and passion for the scene they are creating.

You see this improv rule does not call for aimless action. On the contrary, all gestures and expressions have a purpose on stage—namely to advance the premise to it's best conclusion and to make the dialogue come alive. Energy is never wasted. It is harnessed to propel the ideas into the minds of audience members and engage them more viscerally in the plot.

For example, if an improv actor discovers a four-leafed clover on stage, she does not merely say, "Oh look! There's a four-leafed clover." She walks over, looks down carefully, bends over, picks the imaginary "flower," then, holding it up by the stem, exclaims, "Look what I found. It's a four-leafed clover." She may go on to smell it or put it in her lapel, even if it has nothing more to do with the plot for now. All of these actions enhance the realism of the scene and allow the actor and the audience to have more insight into the character she is portraying.

Everyday Practice

What has this improv rule got to do with real life? Plenty! If you and I spent as much time actually doing what we say we're going to do as we spend talking about it, life would change dramatically. This rule is the quintessential example of "walking your talk." When you act out your ideas, they grow and expand. Others are attracted to the energy.

Here's a simple example. As you ask your grandchildren to clean up their toys, you tell them that if they do a good job, you will get each one a cookie. Great idea! It should motivate them. Want to add power to your words? Go first to the cookie jar. Take out a cookie for each grandchild. Walk into the playroom and, while holding up the cookies, announce, "I have a cookie here for every grandchild who cleans up his toys, and the biggest one goes to whoever does it fastest."

Those gestures will supercharge your words to the point that you'll probably inspire a grand*father* to dive into the clean up effort as well.

Returning one last time to your hypothetical diabetes problem, you have now collaborated successfully with your doctor to reach a diagnosis and then to develop a competent and comprehensive management plan. Great job so far.

However, your ultimate success depends on yet another ingredient: your personal execution of the plan. You must be the one who "acts out" the dietary restrictions, the exercise program and the monitoring process. If you do not put your best intentions into action, you will fall short of the best result.

Improv Exercise

The improv game called Freeze Tag is an excellent vehicle for demonstrating the power of acting things out. You need a pretty good sized group to play it, so you might have to sign up for one of my workshops, or invite a lot of people to your next party.. Here's how Freeze Tag goes.

Seven or eight players are chosen to make up the freeze tag team. Two of the players are selected to begin a scene together. The audience assigns them each a character or role, places them in a setting and describes the situation. Working on their "assignment," the two actors begin a scene. They are encouraged to include as much physical action in their dialogue as possible.

The rest of the freeze tag team stands in the background watching the scene carefully for opportunities to yell, "Freeze!" When the two principle actors hear "Freeze," they must do just that—stop in mid action and mid sentence and hold whatever posture or pose they are in. The team member who yelled, "Freeze" approaches the pair and "tags" one of them on the shoulder. The tagged actor is dismissed from the scene and rejoins the rest of the team. The new actor assumes the same body position as her recently dismissed colleague, and then takes the scene in an entirely new direction. The remaining "partner" of the original acting pair must now go along with the new direction, completely letting go of whatever was transpiring in the first scene.

The new direction prevails until another team member yells, "Freeze," tags a colleague, replaces him, and takes the scene in yet another direction. This process repeats again and again for the duration of the game. Team players are encouraged to yell, "Freeze" as soon as they draw an inspiration from watching the movements or postures of their colleagues. They are instructed not to wait until they have a complete plan in mind. The spontaneous impulse to replace a colleague and start the scene off in a different direction is sufficient to "open the door" for fresh creativity. Hanging back destroys this game, which thrives on spontaneous and dramatic action.

For example, suppose the first two actors are assigned the roles of performers in the musical "Oklahoma." As the male actor begins to sing, "Oh, what a beautiful morning," he spreads his arms wide at shoulder height, while his partner watches him adoringly. "Freeze!" shouts a team member. Both actors become frozen in mid gesture and mid song. The shouter tags the shoulder of the "singer," who is dismissed, and then assumes the same posture with arms spread wide. He says, "Yep, it was the biggest fish I ever caught. Must have been this big from head to tail!" The other actor responds, "What kind of bait did you use?" "Oh, it was just one of these squiggly fat worms," he answers, placing an imaginary live worm in her hand, as she makes a squeamish expression. "Freeze!' rings out. Again both actors become like statues, frozen in mid action. The team member who shouted, tags the fisherman, assumes his position of placing the worm in the other's hand, and says, "With this ring, I thee wed."

You get the picture. In a flash this game takes us from a Broadway musical stage, to an exaggerated fish tale, and then into a wedding ceremony with a very squeamish bride. It's fast moving and fun, all based on action, trust and flexibility. Of course another improv rule is in force as well. The actor not "tagged" must remain in her "old" position, but at the same time be ready to adapt immediately to the new premise, no matter how attached she might have been to the last one.

Can you imagine how energizing it would be if you were consistently surrounded and supported by people who were this flexible and spontaneous, regardless of the circumstances? Can you further imagine how successful you could be, if you were one of them?

5. DO YOUR BEST

Now we come to the improv rule that literally determines the difference between a good performance and a great one. Maximum effort produces maximum results. It's so simple, it's a wonder we even have to bring it up. Yet, time and again we see examples in life of giving less than a best effort: the distracted check out clerk at the supermarket who never makes eye contact; the professional athlete dispassionately going through the motions of his craft; the contractor who builds it just good enough to be "up to code."

When you are giving less than your best effort, you are lacking in passion, and, without passion, you have no hope of reaching the heights of success or happiness you yearn for. Why would you want to give a half-hearted effort? Remember, when it comes to the heart first strategies you're practicing, there is no middle ground. Your heart is either 100% committed, or it's not involved at all.

Yes, we all have given less than our best at times for a variety of reasons. It's important to recognize that when this happens it is not good for us. We are cheating ourselves as well as others. Therefore it behooves us to keep this kind of experience to the bare minimum in our lives.

As we can see so clearly on the improv stage, when a person is obviously giving 100%, it makes her performance better, inspires her acting colleagues to do the same, and evokes an even stronger "rooting interest" from the audience. Passion is often even more compelling than content.

Everyday Practice

Maybe you've heard of Ben Comen. A few years ago he was a member of the cross-country team at Hanna High School in Anderson, South Carolina. He never won a race. In fact, he never came close to winning a race. Whereas most of the other runners finished the 3.1-mile long races in 30 minutes or less, Ben's average time was 51 minutes. Was he a failure? You tell me.

You see Ben has cerebral palsy. The disease leaves his mind clear as a bell, but messes up his coordination and balance something fierce. Consequently he would stumble through every race like a Times Square drunk on a ten day binge, falling heavily and often, but always getting back up and going on. It was at times painful to watch him run.

Nevertheless, Ben finished every race he started, no matter how long it took him. And every time he crossed the finish line he had lots of company. His own teammates would go back out on the course to run the last ten minutes with him. So would most of the opposing team, along with the cheerleaders. Parents and fellow students waited for him at the finish line to applaud and cheer, if they could find their voices through the lumps in their throats.

Why did he do it? The answer is in his own words: "You can either stop trying or you can pick yourself up and keep going. It's just more fun to keep going." Can there be a more powerful example of doing your best than Ben Comen? Was he a success? You tell me.

Improv Exercise

There is no single improv game or exercise that emphasizes this rule more than any other. It is profoundly integral to all of them. So, go over the exercises we've already described and practice them each again with an emphasis on giving everything you've got to every minute of participation. Make sure you're holding nothing back.

6. CELEBRATE ALL PROGRESS

We have a natural tendency to wait until a job is done before we celebrate our accomplishments. Nobody wants to get caught "counting her chickens" too soon. Celebrating all progress flies directly in the face of that conventional tendency, because for improvisation success, the process and the people are *always* more significant than the final product. Thus, it makes sense to focus upon each small step in the improv process and on the behaviors that encourage and support continued creative risk-taking.

It's like taking on a jigsaw puzzle. Sure, you can wait until it's completely assembled before you "ooh and aah" over it. But, I guarantee you'll have more fun and experience more enthusiasm if you exclaim over the placement of each piece along the way. We just simply do better and go further when we have frequent positive reinforcement.

On the improv stage, all the rules you've learned have one overriding objective: to move the scene along. This one is no exception. Because there is no script, no one really knows what the outcome is supposed to be. Each actor thinks of possibilities, but knows that the scene can't go in all possible directions at once. The development of any scene coalesces around the actors mutually discovering and celebrating each "puzzle piece" as it falls into place. The discovery process is itself a form of celebration and accounts for much of the energy we witness and feel, as we watch the performance.

Another form of celebration on stage is seen in the way the "team" honors and respects each actor's input. This, as opposed to more obvious celebration behavior (i.e. "high-fiving" or applauding), is the more likely way that improvisers celebrate and encourage one another on the stage.

Everyday Practice

By following this rule in real life, you are not compromising your standards. You are increasing your chances of meeting them. You can hold onto your most ambitious goals and still celebrate every step you take toward reaching them. You and those around you will only draw more energy and encouragement from your interim celebrations.

This rule ensures continued success, by focusing you on the "glass half full," rather than the "glass half empty." You may have a concern that celebrating your progress in losing weight might tempt you to stop your efforts and "rest on your laurels" prematurely, for example. In truth, however, celebrating the loss is more likely to encourage your continuing effort by recognizing your accomplishment and rewarding you for it. By the way, it doesn't preclude another celebration when you *do* reach your ideal weight.

Expressing gratitude daily for the people who are supporting you is another form of celebrating on your part. For their part, it will only serve to sustain their commitment to you over time. And, of course, you'll have greater success if you can keep your human support system enthusiastic and intact.

Improv Exercise

The best way to demonstrate the powerful potential of this

improv rule is to play a simple game I call "Positive Bounce." You need only two people to play, although it can be expanded to include as many as you like.

Person #1 listens while Person #2 describes something positive from her current life—something good that has happened or something she's proud of. As #1 listens intently, she keeps repeating over and over, "That's great. Tell me more." This goes on for about two minutes, and then the roles are reversed. Now #1 shares from her life, while #2 listens, repeating the words, "That's great. Tell me more."

Now, if you considered this game with your mind only, you wouldn't think much of it. You might even say, "That sounds silly—all that contrived enthusiasm!"

However, if you actually submit yourself to it (as in, accept the "silly" premise), you will find that your heart soon takes over, and your heart knows it's not silly. As you might expect, the person who is sharing the good thing from her life, becomes more and more enthusiastic and encouraged every time she hears, "That's great." But that's only half the story.

Here's the surprising part. If you are the one who keeps asking to hear more, you become filled with energy and enthusiasm as well. The game lifts both players equally. Pretty amazing results from a "silly," mindless exercise, huh? If you have already begun following these improv rules, you're probably not at all surprised.

So, now you know the secrets to great improvisation. Of course, the biggest secret of all is that your level of talent is practically irrelevant. What counts is your level of passion and commitment to practicing the strategies and tactics you have learned.

You have everything you need.

If you are now willing to put your whole heart into it, you can be happier and healthier right this minute.

Post Script: Keeping It Fresh

Last Sunday my son Greg planned to rinse his car off, take a bike ride with his three sons while it dried, and wax it when the four of them returned. He carefully positioned his two older sons with his two-year-old on their walkway and gave them instructions to keep the younger boy from running onto the driveway. Then he backed his car out of the garage to move it closer to the hose.

As he backed up, Greg's eyes were fixed on his three sons to make sure they were all safely off the driveway. When he turned out of the garage, he heard a loud scraping noise.

His two older sons were staring, gape-jawed at the front of the car. "Dad, what happened?"

Greg got out to look. He had scraped the right front of his car against the garage door wall, and his bumper was now sitting on the driveway.

Greg could have chosen from a number of options in reacting to this situation. He could have beaten himself up for his "dumb" mistake. He could have gotten angry at the unnecessary cost and inconvenience he had just created for himself. He could have begun worrying about how much this would cost to repair.

Guess what he did?

He smiled, told the boys that everything was going to be fine, and took them on the bike ride they had planned. When he got home, he tied the bumper onto the car's frame, and called his wife. "Honey, remember the front bumper with the scrape and gouge that we've been putting off getting repaired? Well, we're going to get it repaired this week." The two of them chuckled about that.

Greg went on to have a great day with his kids. Every time he was tempted to get mad, worried, or afraid, he reminded himself to stay in the present moment. He refused to beat himself up or second-guess himself and he refused to worry about the potential problems of repairing his car.

That, my friends, is a fully functioning humor nature in action—toned and well oiled. Does Greg respond to every situation in the same manner? Of course not. But I can guarantee you that with the commitment he's made to using the amazing natural medicine of humor, he always has the choice to function at that level.

You have the same choice. You can have unhappiness if you want it, but you can also evaluate your options and choose to be happy instead.

Now that you have begun having your own experiences applying your life to humor, if you have not already felt its transforming power, you soon will. With humor you are becoming free from your old habits of stress, worry, unease, and unhappiness. With humor you are finding inner peace and greater self-confidence. With humor, in fact, you are beginning to see your world differently—with eyes you've not used in many, many years.

And as your personal growth continues, you are discovering that your powerful humor nature has always been with you and available to you. You can easily recall times, even while deeply influenced by seriousness, when you found relief and refuge in humor. Now the day has come when you can use your humor nature as you were born to use it.

You have survived your seriousness long enough to be

reintroduced to your humor nature and to become reacquainted with its amazing natural medicinal potency. Humor's vitality now satiates your body, mind, and spirit, guiding your attitudes and actions, and showing you how to live happily.

But please understand this does not mean that your seriousness will shrivel up and blow away. You have a deeply ingrained propensity to get serious when presented with an emotional, or high stakes, situation. Your brain is not like a computer; you can't simply erase an old program and install a new one in its place. These changes you've engaged are real and valid, but they will not become permanent without continued effort on your part.

Sometimes you will find yourself caught up in old ideas. The siren call of seriousness will be especially tempting when you have a lot at stake. Don't be discouraged. Seriousness is pervasive and insidious and you've practiced it for almost all of your adult life. You got pretty darn good at it so it's only natural that it will be a hard habit to break.

What situations stress you out? Is your baby crying in the back seat of your car during a long trip? Are you faced with a deadline on something important, with lots of people paying attention? I'm sure you have other, perhaps more powerful, images you can conjure that make it very difficult for you to be happy.

You're not after happiness only when it's easy or convenient—anyone can do that. Humor is powerful enough to help you shine during your toughest circumstances. But, it is up to you to keep your humor nature fresh, even when the chips are down.

When seriousness rears its ugly head, you must remember the smile strategies. They are the keys to your freedom. Giving in to your seriousness is an old thinking pattern that will diminish with time and practice. But you cannot afford to be complacent because the potential for seriousness exists during every waking moment. You must keep your commitment fresh and strong every day.

Several years ago I accompanied the revived Broadway musical, "Damn Yankees" to several of the cities on its American tour. This gave me the opportunity to attend more than fifty performances of that wonderful show. You'd think that, with that great script and music that have won so many awards, successful performances would be assured every single night. Well, not exactly.

It became clear to me that, for the show to sparkle night after night, the cast had to find a way to make fresh the words and lyrics that had stood the test of thousands of successful performances—as though they were performing them for the first time.

Sometimes they did it by changing the inflection of a word or two in a critical speech. At other times, they played mischievous tricks on one another from the wings of the stage (unseen by the audience, of course). On occasion, members of the cast would switch minor parts. Once they even dressed me up and "smuggled" me on stage during a crowd scene, just to give the lead performer an extra challenge to "stay in character."

I'm told this is the same challenge faced by all professional performers who want to avoid relying on yesterday's accolades. If this is necessary for the sustained success of talented people in the theatre, I think it is mandatory for any of us who seek the same level of success in our lives.

To help you achieve this "freshness," I have developed seven tips. They will keep your daily focus squarely upon my smile strategies and your newly reinvigorated lightness and happiness.

TIP NUMBER ONE: RECYCLE YOURSELF

Once you have spent a year focusing on my smile strategies, one week at a time, you deserve a celebration. In fact, you'll be throwing one for yourself every day just based upon your improved health and success. Remember, however, that you're having a celebration... not a graduation. Even when seriousness is in remission, it does not go away.

Make sure that your celebration includes getting back to basics by starting anew with the first smile strategy and enjoying each of them all over again. You'll be amazed at the new meaning you uncover during your second time through...and your third...and your fourth. The lessons you glean will broaden in scope because of your accumulated experience—you're building upon a solid foundation of success.

Tonya, a patient, admitted that she initially treated my smile strategies like "homework." She wanted to do them, but she wasn't quite ready to drop all her routines of seriousness. Most of us are like Tonya, we don't wake up every morning looking for ways we can change ourselves. You enjoy your routines because, even when they're painful or unproductive, they provide you with predictability.

But your routines of seriousness were slowly killing you, just like Tonya's were doing her in. And what Tonya found was that by recycling herself through the smile strategies, she could avoid the trap of the "homework" mentality. Even though she only skimmed the surface the first time through, Tonya discovered she was learning more than she thought. Then she went on to glean much more from her second time. You will too.

TIP NUMBER TWO: BE SELFISH

Have you ever read those instructions on an airplane for the oxygen mask? Even if you're traveling with a small infant, you are told to put the oxygen mask on yourself before you put it on her. Why? Because if you're not healthy and conscious, you're absolutely no help to your small companion. That's right; if you want to help someone else you must be selfish. What good are you to your family if you aren't ensuring your own light attitude? Your stress levels and anxiety will circumvent all your good intentions. Get in the habit of meeting your needs first.

My friend Eunice confronted me one afternoon because, no matter how much she was applying humor, she was still unhappy. Eunice, it turns out, was more focused on helping other people smile than she was in smiling herself. She needed to learn the difference between selfishness and self-centeredness. Selfishness is taking care of yourself so you can help other people, while self-centeredness is taking care of yourself at other's expense. Eunice didn't want to be self-centered, but she needed to learn to be selfish, and so do you.

When you're not taking care of yourself the only victory you'll experience is the passive-aggressive kind—the smug self-righteousness of knowing you sacrificed to help other people. But guess what? Although you might derive some sense of twisted satisfaction from your sacrifice, the fact remains... you still sacrificed yourself! That's unhealthy.

When you follow this tip you're going to notice two simple yet powerful effects: 1. You will be happier and healthier, and 2. You're going to be able to help a lot more people.

TIP NUMBER THREE: TAKE IT ONE DAY AT A TIME

My friend Rob couldn't move beyond using humor for recreation because he was always worried about what he hadn't done yesterday. Or if not, he was usually afraid of what he might not do tomorrow. And like the old saying, with one foot in yesterday and one foot in tomorrow, Rob was missing today!

Rob learned to keep his focus on today, and you should too. After all, using humor merely for recreation is like having a gourmet kitchen and only using it to make peanut butter sandwiches.

Keeping your focus on today negates your resentments about the past and your fears about the future. And today is the only place you're going to find your fun anyway!

TIP NUMBER FOUR: AVOID ISOLATION

A wise mentor once told me, "Self-centeredness is impossible in a vacuum," which means you'll never know where you are having problems with self-centeredness unless you are out participating fully in life. Your mistakes of action, skinning your proverbial knee, are the very things that show you where you need to grow. That's why you should be embracing your mistakes, just as I've taught you to do!

Get out in the world and interact. You'll spot seriousness right away because it'll be found in the areas where you feel things aren't happening "like they're supposed to."

Sandra, a patient, swears by a wonderful, simple, and incredibly effective strategy: she gives a genuine compliment to everyone she meets. It might be a stranger sharing an elevator with her or a client at her workplace, but Sandra finds something about them to express appreciation for. She tells me her formula works like magic. She is never without happy conversation wherever she goes.

She also knows immediately when seriousness is gaining a toehold because, whenever that's happening, she has trouble finding something to compliment. And guess what? Once she spots seriousness, she nips it in the bud.

TIP NUMBER FIVE: FIND YOUR PEOPLE

Over 90% of all heart bypass patients are back to their bad health habits within two years of their surgery. Dr. Dean Ornish, however, has raised the success rate of these types of patients to almost 70% by introducing one simple ingredient—support. Having a support group is not only pleasant and affirming. It can save your life.

Start following the heart patients' lead. Cultivate your own humor support group right now. Identify your members one at a time and share with them how important they are to your health and success. Nourish those relationships like a baby flower bud in the spring.

My patient, Lori, makes a point to find a kindred spirit in every group to which she belongs. Be it a committee at work, a church group, or folks in her neighborhood, Lori's goal is to locate the other person(s) with an active humor nature so she can have a healthy dialogue and ensure a light-hearted attitude no matter what activity she's involved in.

The good news is that these people are usually looking for you too. Don't waste time on people who aren't helping you take yourself more lightly.

TIP NUMBER SIX: DON'T APPLY MY SMILE STRATEGIES TO YOUR LIFE

You read that correctly; you mustn't apply my smile strategies to your life. Because they constitute a new way of living, you must apply your life to my smile strategies. You'll find this new way of life so abundant and pleasing you'll wonder how you made do without humor for so long. You will always stay fresh if you adhere to this tip because humor is all about seeing life with a fresh eye.

My friend Carla thought she was already getting the most out of humor, but she was really only applying humor to her life. To be sure, she could always be counted on to ease the tension of a difficult moment with a witty and on-target remark. However, when her mother died suddenly, it made her realize how helpless she truly was in the face of seriousness and unhappiness.

Given the gift of desperation, she began to apply her life in earnest to the smile strategies. "I used to force a smile onto my face all the time," she remembers. "Now I have learned to live my smile and make every action consistent with it. Before, I was always looking for surprises. Now

I treat every moment as a surprise and a gift. And where I previously made humor by challenging all assumptions, I now find that I'm living more by faith and making fewer assumptions to begin with."

This has made an amazing difference in Carla. She has been transformed from a person who was *funny to have around* into one who is *fun to be around.* She finds true joy in everyday things.

This is exactly why many of my cancer and chronic pain patients wind up telling me that their disease is actually a blessing. Their diagnosis constitutes a "loaded gun," without which they might never have found a new, happy way of life through humor. Now that you have read this book, I trust you won't have to wait for such intense motivation.

Humor is not, after all, high-octane fuel for your engine; humor *is* your engine.

TIP NUMBER SEVEN: GIVE BACK

If you want to learn something in a way you'll never forget, simply teach it to someone else. Since you'll never forget what you impart to someone else, I want you to teach others about humor's amazing natural medicine.

Actively seek someone to mentor. Start teaching a smile strategy group in your church or at your community center. Humor is a popular topic. It is being utilized to help people do everything from relaxation to losing weight. You'll find people receptive to your teachings.

They'll be especially receptive when they see you embodying the very things you're purporting to teach them.

These freshness tips will help you be vigilant for stress, worry, fear, and unhappiness—those uncomfortable feelings you get when things seem like they're happening all wrong. Treat these undesirable feelings as symptoms, just like you would treat pain in your big toe as a symptom that you've gotten a splinter. And treat your symptoms of seriousness the same way you would that splinter: pluck them out, using my smile strategies.

One sure sign that seriousness is creeping back into your life is the feeling that you've become distant from other people. If you find yourself feeling inferior, superior, or different from the people around you, you are isolating yourself. Such separation from the spirit of friendship and community slows your humor nature to the speed of molasses.

You have learned to value the love and respect of others and, in turn, you've seen how valuable you are to the people around you. As you become more humor-reliant and gain more self-respect, you realize that you can't afford to separate yourself from people. You don't want to short-change them, or you. You now know that your real value is in simply being yourself because you are perfect just as you are.

By allowing humor to guide your life, you become able to truly add value to other's lives. You find yourself able to love others unconditionally, and to share your joy openly, because you are merely expressing outwardly how you feel about yourself.

Let's face it, your mental and emotional functions, such as your ability to love and your ability to express your feelings, were greatly affected by your seriousness. Your stress levels were too high to allow deep and rewarding happiness, serenity, and joy. Your spirit, in a manner of speaking, was broken.

It's fixed now.

Welcome home. In time, through your commitment to humor, your life can be filled with true beauty. Perhaps you won't become rich or famous, although I know many people who've used the amazing power of humor to do just that. I can guarantee you this: Drawing upon the unfailing energy of your humor nature to live abundantly will allow you to be happier than you have ever been before.